£4.25

To

# ANTHOLOGIE ÉLUARD

# METHUEN'S TWENTIETH CENTURY
# FRENCH TEXTS

*Founder Editor:* W.J. STRACHAN, M.A. (1959–78)
*General Editor:* J.E. FLOWER

ANOUILH: *L'Alouette* ed. Merlin Thomas and Simon Lee
BAZIN: *Vipère au poing* ed. W.J. Strachan
BERNANOS: *Nouvelle Histoire de Mouchette* ed. Blandine Stefanson
CAMUS: *La Chute* ed. B.G. Garnham
CAMUS: *L'Étranger* ed. Germaine Brée and Carlos Lynes
CAMUS: *La Peste* ed. W.J. Strachan
CAMUS: *Selected Political Writings* ed. J.H. King
DURAS: *Moderato cantabile* ed. W.J. Strachan
DURAS: *Le Square* ed. W.J. Strachan
GENET: *Le Balcon* ed. David H. Walker
GIRAUDOUX: *Electre* ed. Merlin Thomas and Simon Lee
GISCARD D'ESTAING: *Démocratie française* ed. Alan Clark
LAINÉ: *La Dentellière* ed. M.J. Tilby
MAURIAC: *Destins* ed. Colin Thornton–Smith
ROBBE-GRILLET: *La Jalousie* ed. B.G. Garnham
SARTRE: *Huis clos* ed. Jacques Hardré and George Daniel
SARTRE: *Les Jeux sont faits* ed. M.R. Storer
SARTRE: *Les Mains sales* ed. Geoffrey Brereton
SARTRE: *Les Mots* ed. David Nott
TROYAT: *Grandeur nature* ed. Nicholas Hewitt

*Anthologie de contes et nouvelles modernes* ed. Conlon
*Anthologie Éluard* ed. Clive Scott
*Anthologie Prévert* ed. Christiane Mortelier
*Anthology of Second World War French Poetry* ed. Ian Higgins

Paul Éluard

# ANTHOLOGIE ÉLUARD

*Edited by*

**Clive Scott, M.A., M.Phil., D.Phil.(Oxon)**

*Lecturer in the School of*
*Modern Languages and European History*
*University of East Anglia*

Methuen Educational Ltd

*First published in 1983 by*
*Methuen Educational Ltd*
*11 New Fetter Lane, London EC4P 4EE*

*Text © 1968 by Éditions Gallimard*
*Introduction and Notes © 1983 by Clive Scott*

*Printed in Great Britain by Richard Clay,*
*Bungay, Suffolk*

British Library Cataloguing in Publication Data

Éluard, Paul
Anthologie Éluard – (Methuen's twentieth century texts)
Rn: Eugène Grindel   I. Title   II. Scott, Clive
841'.912      PQ2609.L75

ISBN  0–423–50880–6

# CONTENTS

The editor and publishers are grateful
to Éditions Gallimard for permission
to reproduce the poems in this collection.

# LIST OF POEMS

## 2 AMATORY

3  PICTORIAL

4  ANIMAL

# INTRODUCTION

Paul Éluard was born Eugène-Émile-Paul Grindel at Saint-Denis on 14 December 1895; he only assumed the name we know him by – the maiden-name of his maternal grandmother – in 1914. Éluard's childhood was a comfortable one; he attended the *école communale* at Saint-Denis and then at Aulnay-sous-Bois, where the family subsequently moved. In 1908, the Grindels established themselves in Paris and took to spending their summer holidays in Switzerland, at Glion near Montreux.

It was at this resort that in July 1912 Éluard fell seriously ill with tuberculosis, which necessitated a lengthy stay at a sanatorium in Clavadel, near Davos (from December 1912 to February 1914). During this convalescence he met and fell in love with the daughter of a Russian lawyer, Helena Dmitrievna Diakonova (Gala). Mobilized in December 1914, Éluard spent most of the war in hospitals, both as a nurse and a patient, and served only briefly at the front as an infantryman. 1917 saw his marriage to Gala and the publication of his first significant poems, *Le Devoir et l'inquiétude*, which he had issued in a limited roneotyped edition in 1916 as *Le Devoir*. In the following year his daughter, Cécile, was born and *Poèmes pour la paix* were published. These two war collections bear witness to Éluard's painfully learned pacifist convictions and are filled with pleas for that tranquil, domestic happiness of which he was to remain so eloquent an apologist.

On his demobilization in May 1919, he was introduced by Jean Paulhan to the Dadaists of the *Littérature* group (Breton, Soupault, Aragon – Tzara arrived in Paris in January 1920) and took part in most of their 'events' of 1920, the year in which he founded his own short-lived review, *Proverbe* (five numbers), and published another verse-collection, *Les Animaux et leurs hommes, les hommes et leurs animaux* illustrated by André Lhôte. With Picabia's[1] withdrawal from the Dadaists in 1921 and the rupture between Breton and Tzara in 1922, the *Littérature* group went its own way, towards Surrealism, as Dada withered away. On the 24 March 1924, just before the publication of *Mourir de ne pas mourir*, Éluard, apparently subject to a loss of faith in his own literary identity, set off without warning on a journey round the world. In the meantime, Surrealism took firmer shape, and Breton's first Surrealist manifesto appeared in November. Éluard had returned to Paris in October and immediately threw himself into the collaborative work of the Surrealists, making the acquaintance of Picasso and giving lodging to Max Ernst, whom he had first met in 1921. The Moroccan rebellion of 1925 drew the Surrealists into revolutionary politics, and Aragon, Breton and Éluard joined the Communist Party in 1926, the year of publication of *Capitale de la douleur*. Éluard returned to a sanatorium in the winter of 1928, at Arosa, and during his stay, corrected the proofs of *L'Amour la poésie*, which appeared the following year. 1929 was a year of changing partners: Desnos, Leiris, Queneau and Prévert left the Surrealists, Buñuel, Char and Dali joined; Gala left Éluard, for Dali, whom she later married, while Éluard turned his affections to Maria Benz (Nusch), an actress, who became his wife in 1934.

The separation of Éluard and Gala took place in 1930, the year of Breton's second manifesto and of Tzara's return to the fold, and of the collaborative works *Ralentir travaux*

(Éluard, Breton and Char) and *L'Immaculée Conception* (prose-poems, Éluard and Breton). On the political front, the early 1930s also brought changes of allegiance and emphasis. Aragon and Georges Sadoul, as official representatives of French Surrealism, attended the Second International Congress of Revolutionary Writers at Kharkov in November 1930; back in Paris, Aragon sought to intensify the politicization of Surrealism, and was taxed with betrayal of the group by Éluard in the strikingly vehement pamphlet *Certificat* of 1932; Aragon and Sadoul quitted the Surrealists, while Breton and Éluard were excluded from the Communist Party (1933). But this latter event in no way diminished their political commitment: throughout the 1930s, Breton and Éluard pursued their left-wing sympathies and relentlessly attacked fascism in all its forms, particularly as it manifested itself in the Spanish Civil War. The signs of Éluard's developing sense of public responsibility are to be found in the collections *Cours naturel* (1938) and *Donner à voir* (1939). But it was in 1938, also, that the flame of Surrealism made its final leap, with the *Exposition Internationale du Surréalisme*, Galerie des Beaux-Arts, in January, and died, as Breton and Éluard parted company, ostensibly because Éluard had had enough of Surrealism's bad faith and lack of seriousness, and because Breton felt that Éluard took his communist sympathies too far.

After the outbreak of the Second World War and the subsequent armistice and demobilization of June 1940, Éluard turned all his energies to the Resistance, pacifism no longer being a possibility. Living in semi-secrecy, always on the move, changing his name, Éluard asked to be readmitted to the proscribed Communist Party (1942) and produced a tireless sequence of subversive protest poems, in which the celebration of love became a celebration of the solidarity of all the oppressed (*Livre ouvert II*, 1942; *Poésie et vérité 1942*, 1942; *Les Sept Poèmes d'amour en guerre*, 1943; *Le Lit la table*, 1944; *Les Armes de la douleur*, 1944; *Au rendez-vous allemand*, 1944). In these war years, the coordination of the literary resistance focused in the *Comité National des Écrivains*, which Éluard helped to organize and in which figures such as Paulhan, Leiris, Aragon, Triolet, Desnos played their part. Éluard also prepared two anthologies of Resistance poetry, with the title *L'Honneur des poètes*, to which he contributed under the pseudonyms Maurice Hervent and Jean du Haut; he supplied the preface for the first volume (1943), while Aragon provided that of the second (1944).

After the war, and the pressures of a peculiarly clandestine public function, Éluard felt the need to recover a private self and fully re-enter the world of Nusch (*Lingères légères*, 1945; *Poésie ininterrompue I*, 1946; *Le Dur Désir de durer*, 1946). None the less, Éluard was to be found, in 1946, lecturing in Prague, interesting himself in the Italian elections, in Milan and Turin, and bringing support to the independence fighters in Greece. And it was again abroad, in Switzerland, that he learnt of Nusch's sudden death from a cerebral haemorrhage (28 November 1946), an event which lies at the heart of the collection *Le Temps déborde* (1947). Éluard was nursed through the months of despair which followed by Jacqueline and Alain Trutat and it was to Jacqueline that the poems of *Corps mémorable* (1947, 1948) were dedicated.

Éluard's political engagement continued unabated: he was involved in the struggle to have the communist victims of McCarthyism freed (1948), and, later, in a campaign to save the Rosenbergs (executed June 1953). While at a Peace Congress in Mexico as a delegate for the World Council of Peace, he met Dominique Lemor, whom he was to marry in 1951, and who is the inspiration of the collection *Le Phénix* (1951): 'Le Phénix, c'est le couple – Adam et Ève – qui est et n'est pas le premier'. But Éluard's new-found fulfilment was cut short by his death, after a heart-attack, on 18 November 1952.

### LITERARY–HISTORICAL

### Dada

Dada came into being in Zürich, in 1916 ('dada' is, variously, a child's first utterance, the Romanian for 'yes', the French for a hobby-horse), at the Cabaret Voltaire, out of the combined efforts of Hugo Ball, Richard Huelsenbeck, Hans Arp, Tristan Tzara and others. Marcel Duchamp and Francis Picabia were already engaging in outrageous Dada-like activities in New York, and other cities became centres of Dada after the war: Cologne, Berlin, Paris. Dada was a howl of disgust against a society atrophied by servility to capitalist commercialism, rationality, repressive moralities, élitisms. Borrowing its artistic methods eclectically – collage from Cubism, 'words-in-freedom' and 'noise-sound'[2] from Futurism, for example – Dada sought both to undermine museum commodity-art by absorbing some of its features into expressly auto-destructive artistic practices, and to promote a new art which was primitive and imbued with the 'unreasonable' patterns of nature, an anonymous art, corporately produced. Thus, on the one hand was a savagely ironic, stubbornly elusive, never less than heretical Dada (Tzara, Picabia, Duchamp) and on the other, a Dada of a quieter, more idealistic and more consistent hue (Ball, Arp). In language, Dada exploited absurdity as a means of linguistic purification, seeking the enlivened sense that words have in nonsense: words used with a sensitive carelessness recover a primal authenticity, release long-suppressed energies and become part of the cosmic psyche. Éluard's Dadaist phase is to be traced to those collections marked by the influence of Jean Paulhan, *Les Animaux et leurs hommes,...* (1920) and *Les Nécessités de la vie et les conséquences des rêves* (1921), and to his first collaborative work with Max Ernst, *Répétitions* (1922).[3]

## Surrealism

Common to Dada and Surrealism was a conception of themselves as total states of mind, the *artistic* expression of which had no special privilege, indeed was unnecessary: such states could more properly make themselves manifest in multimedia 'events' or 'happenings'. Dada and Surrealism also shared a belief in the profound and liberating aptness of chance, seen in the random juxtapositions of words and phrases cut out from newspapers or of ill-assorted objects, and in automatic writing and drawing. Both movements were attracted to proverbial and aphoristic formulations (see, for instance, Éluard's *152 Proverbes mis au goût du jour*, 1925, written with Benjamin Péret), because aphorisms are the point at which logic and fantasy, rational syntax and semantic game-playing, come to terms with each other; and because they may be infinitely rewritten, showing untiring disregard for authority and the power to remake our understanding of the world in the changing of a single word – originality in the very practice of plagiarism.

While retaining much of Dada's stylistic eclecticism, Surrealism was altogether more systematic and coherent – a fact made clear by André Breton remaining central to its development. It was more exclusively orientated towards the Freudian unconscious, although accounts of dreams were not designed to invite psychoanalysis so much as to generate further dreaming, or moments of self-recognition, in the reader/spectator. Surrealism sought to inhabit the flux of the psyche and to show how it extended over the same space and time as waking consciousness. The Surrealist universe was also motivated by two impulsive and unpredictable forces, desire and chance: desire emerging from deep in the primordial self has a magical way of projecting into external reality the conditions of its fulfilment; this paradoxical phenomenon of preordained coincidence, of *inevitable* chance, was 'le hasard objectif', and elective love was another manifestation of it. The Surrealist image, too, is essentially a chance encounter, of radically different realities, whose electrical charge is directly proportional to that difference, springing from sources beyond knowledge, reshaping perception, and releasing the imagination across infinite associative spaces. Surrealism's 'surreality' was thus not situated in a transcendent realm, but in the human mind itself, an 'au-delà immanent', and the child and the lunatic, with their peculiar availability to the sollicitations of the 'merveilleux', with their spiritual malleability, belonged to Surrealism's 'chosen' people.

There are perhaps ways in which Éluard stands apart from Surrealism. His lyricism publicizes the fact that it belongs to a time-honoured tradition, and its quietness and deliberateness have little to do with the aggressions of the Surrealist imagination and the purely disturbing effects of shock. His poetry often situates itself, it is true, in the realm of dream, but Éluard's dream landscapes have a peculiar sense of purpose, lexical consistency and thematic coherence: there is no anarchy or quirkiness in his vision, indeed the more we read of him, the less we feel the presence of chance. And although Éluard admits that images have a life of their own, he qualifies this autonomy:

> L'image par analogie (ceci est *comme* cela) et l'image par identification (ceci *est* cela) se détachent aisément du poème, tendent à devenir poèmes elles-mêmes, en s'isolant. A moins que les deux termes ne s'enchevêtrent aussi étroitement l'un que l'autre à tous les éléments du poème. (*Premières vues anciennes*, 1937)

This *enchevêtrement* (entanglement) of the terms of the image in the overall lexical texture of the poem, is also, in Éluard's case, an *enchevêtrement* of the image in a presiding tone of voice. Éluard frequently achieves the anonymity of the enraptured medium and of the popular poet, but never far away is the controlling smoothness, the guileless gravity of a familiar voice.

## MORAL AND POLITICAL

Éluard has no doubts about the moral nature of poetry: in a radio broadcast on Charles Baudelaire, in 1949, he describes the poet (in general) as a 'personne morale par excellence'. And an axiom much used by Éluard – 'Le poète est celui qui inspire bien plus que celui qui est inspiré' – emphasizes the propulsive power of the poet: it is the poet who propels the public along the trajectory of its desires for happiness, justice, peace by reflecting these perhaps unconscious desires and making them coherent. But before confidently accepting such a proposition, we should also listen to some of Éluard's prefatory remarks to his collection *Une leçon de morale* (1950):

> Combien de fois ai-je changé l'ordre de ces poèmes, remis au bien ce qui était au mal, et inversement?.... Mes vertus, mes défauts, mon optimisme et mon ineptitude s'enchevêtrent, je suis un homme.... Je me suis voulu moraliste.

Here are to be found doubts, a sense of inextricably enmeshed contrary impulses, an acknowledgement that because opposites are identical the inversion of values is a continual possibility. In fact, Éluard's moralism is more an instinctive drive than a system, and, for three reasons, the reader may profit little from trying to discover a constitutive ideology beneath the moral stance. First, Éluard's 'ideological' utterances are in the form of maxims, and their rhetorical effectiveness depends on begging questions about truth, justice and happiness. Second, Éluard's ineradicably dialectical way of thinking, of which the habit of inversion is a clear symptom, means that moral polarization simply cannot be experienced as schism or dilemma. The dynamism of dialectic releases Éluard into the promise of progress and solution, and this is why he can confidently call poetry a 'langage chargé d'espoir, même quand il est désespéré', because, given that dynamism, there is no reason not to hope. It is hardly surprising that, in a speech on Victor Hugo, delivered on 26 February 1952, Éluard should draw attention to Hugo's predilection for patterns of antithesis and should comment: 'Il n'y a pas de quoi rire de cette méthode d'opposition, de contradiction qui permet toujours à l'homme d'espérer.' Third, moral notions in Éluard tend constantly to shade into existential ones; in other words, however firm Éluard's conceptions of good and evil may be at any time, they are subject to, and are even made irrelevant by, the far greater principle of life itself. Sheer positive living is a 'moral' affirmation more significant than any virtuous action; and, correspondingly, the force of evil lies not so much in wickedness as in all forms of resignation or fatalism.

It was the First World War that first urged a moral *prise de position* on Éluard. All the poems of *Le Devoir et l'inquiétude* were written at the front between August 1916 and July 1917. But Éluard's war poems, in fact, justify themselves by operating beyond the reach of the war, and when the war does impinge, the poet finds himself adopting an apologetic, confessional attitude. In these poems there is no note of self-righteous indignation, nor attacks on the incomprehension of those not involved in the fighting. 'Paris si gai!' is no bitter indictment of the self-absorbed pleasure-seekers on the home front; the poet may speak of the hardships of war, of his own dirtiness, but it is without bias. On the contrary, Paris's very virtues lie in its being untouched by war and in its refusal to deny its own effervescent day-by-day existence. It is, rather, those who pass through Paris and seek their treasure in hidden places, with the plough, who are beyond comprehension; the diamonds of Paris are there, visible, for the taking. Hope, as 'Fidèle' (p. 49) makes clear, is a keeping faith with those left behind in 'ordinary' life, which is the only life.

The other collection growing directly from Éluard's early war experience, the eleven short poems of *Poèmes pour la paix* (1918), are poems of return to the domestic hearth and to Gala, celebrations of the recovered usefulness of the body. War, now only on the distant fringe of consciousness, acts as that unknown which has driven the poet more intensely into the known, resurrecting the riches of the banal.

The First World War was still a war fought on battlefields by soldiers, a war in a world of its own beyond the reach of normality. The Second World War, more thoroughly civilian, created situations in occupied countries in which normality could seem both treachery and rebellion, an over-willingness to make the best of things and a refusal to be driven out of one's humanity. It is upon this unnerving borderline that a poem like Éluard's 'Couvre-feu' (p. 52) locates itself (see Appendix III). But ultimately this is a poem of Resistance, where the poetry itself is the resistance, where language, even reduced to a minimum, wriggles free of constraints and opens up semantic freedoms.

But Éluard is not always to be consoled by language's ability to envelop the event and make it the servant of human continuity. Some events leave language turning in its own circle, unable to absorb them. In his lecture on occasional poetry, 'La poésie de circonstance', delivered in Moscow in 1952, Éluard affirms:

> La circonstance extérieure doit coïncider avec la circonstance intérieure, comme si le poète lui-même l'avait produite. Elle devient donc aussi vraie que l'émotion amoureuse, que la fleur enfantée par le printemps, que la joie de construire pour vivre.

Such a project may be realized in 'Couvre-feu', but 'Critique de la poésie' (p. 53) is a 'critique' precisely because it presents the non-coincidence of bare external events – the deaths at the hands of the enemy of the Spanish poet García Lorca, the French poet Saint-Pol-Roux, and the Resistance-worker Decour, and the torture of Saint-Pol-Roux's daughter – and poetic reflection. This is, in fact, the second poem with this title: an earlier 'Critique de la poésie', first published in 1931, appeared in *La Vie immédiate* (1932) and calls the reader to share the poet's violent hatred of the bourgeoisie, the rule of law and order, and clericalism. It ends with the lines:

> Je crache à la face de l'homme plus petit que nature
> Qui à tous mes poèmes ne préfère pas cette *Critique de la poésie*.

What Éluard seems to be regretting here are the inevitable interferences of poetic artifice, which, while empowering the poet to push constantly beyond his own limits, compelling him to re-invent his language, prevent him from transmitting, unadorned, a totally committed response to the external world. The poem must fight a running battle against its own poeticization and its consequent loss of an elementary audacity. The expansive, prosodic looseness of these last two lines, one of fifteen syllables, the other of twenty-two, discloses a poet who sometimes wishes that poetry would relax into the dimensions of his own voice.

Éluard's dissatisfactions with poetry in the second 'Critique de la poésie' are rather different. The first stanza is dominated by fire and forest, images of conflagration and refreshment, the luminous and the vegetable. It is a stanza from which the first person is absent, and to understand the import of this, we should refer to the two sentences following those already quoted from 'La poésie de circonstance':

> Le poète suit son idée, mais cette idée le mène à s'inscrire dans la courbe du progrès humain. Et, petit à petit, le monde le remplace, le monde chante à travers lui.

The first person effaces itself in its role of medium as the world finds its own path through the poet; the poet is a collective being whose name happens to be Éluard.[4] Thus objects, multiplied and unpossessed, possess each other:

> Les troncs les cœurs les mains les feuilles

and, in their unification, release a happiness which is all pure quality, richly diverse and divorced from any object:

> Confus léger fondant sucré

But the simply stated fact:

> García Lorca a été mis à mort

remains unassimilated and unassimilable; the murder of the poet by General Franco's men halts progress and paralyses the movement of *affabulation*. The death of Lorca is an historical event which arrests history; the present tense of the first stanza is nullified by the passive perfect tense, the past which reverberates forward and cancels a future.

Where the first stanza approaches fusion, through conflagration, the third approaches it through liquefaction: light is no longer related to a source, the sun, but is everywhere evident in the enveloping translucence of water; the fountains of the first stanza are no longer created by the light, but by the human figure, dispensing light through them. The tears of the child are not tears of pain ('sans larmes') but a communication of unimpeded vision. But this enterprise of the imagination is equally interrupted by a statement, crushing in its refusal to be anything other than a statement.

And the fifth stanza finally yields to the disintegrative factors already foreshadowed in the third stanza: the perilously solitary child becomes the solitary poet brought back to the prison of the first person; the noun without an article ('maison'), without the sign that gives it identity or places it in a specific destiny (the definite article) and without the sign that fills it with potentiality (the indefinite article), comes to predominate (ville, fleurs, pierres, murs); the inorganic replaces the organic. The poet confesses to escapism. Decour's death seals his failure.

In this poem, then, poetry is unable to make death serve humanity, as a reason for living, is unable to deny the solitude of these victims, and becomes itself another solitude. It is in the arena of politics, of war, that the present threatens to lose its power of revitalization. The present moments of war are moments of anarchy, hiatus, savage rupture, which the poet is powerless to bridge. In his commentary for the film made by Alain Resnais and Robert Hessens in 1950 on the bombing of Guernica, a film using Picasso's canvas as its frame of reference, Éluard wrote:

> Car avec le présent, c'est le passé, c'est le passé et l'avenir qui s'éparpillent, toute une suite qui se rompt, qui se consume, dans une cratère.

Poetry's political effectiveness, the means whereby words

become action, a source of moral rearmament, depends on its not lying, on its reliability as human evidence. 'Critique de la poésie', in the end, has to acknowledge its own hypocrisy. The poem on Gabriel Péri (p. 59), however, has no such needs (see Appendix III).

Perhaps the best summary of Éluard's conception of the 'political' is the title of the first part of his *Poèmes politiques* (1948), namely 'De l'horizon d'un homme à l'horizon de tous'. Just as the love of the couple develops into a pledge of total human solidarity, so the 'revolutionary' element in a poet's language moulds a new social awareness, an awareness of our own perfectibility when constraints and inhibitions are lifted, and of a self-realization to be achieved through self-multiplication – the personal experience of egalitarianism. It would not be wrong to suggest that Éluard's politics are utopian in that they imply an unimaginable mixture of individualism and communism. And it is true that his exhortations too often sound automatic and unquestioning, that he is too insistent on his own exemplariness. But we should certainly not underestimate the importance of the poet in preventing the devaluation of our political vocabulary. The abstract nouns of ideology are by him reinvested with the density of common nouns, and consequently can be repossessed by mankind, for they are now immunized against the manipulative usage of politicians.

### AMATORY

In an anonymous review of *Une longue réflexion amoureuse* (1945), the reviewer wrote:

> *Une longue réflexion amoureuse* ne rompt en aucune façon avec ce que l'on pourrait appeler 'la tradition d'Éluard', ce cheminement d'homme sans effroi, ni heurt, cette révélation presque systématique d'un univers miraculeux qui tient tout entier dans ce mot: amour.

Éluard's moral and political attitudes are generated out of

the same source as all his imaginative energy, the love of the loving couple. The analogies engendered by the mind, the affinities revealed by chance encounter, the kinships of those with a common condition and destiny, all are to be traced back to the very principle of analogy and reciprocity – the loved and loving individual:

> Femme tu mets au monde un corps toujours pareil
> Le tien
>
> Tu es la ressemblance.                    ('Tu te lèves...', p. 73)

The bridge between the loving couple and a larger community is provided by 'Sans âge' (p. 74), a poem which makes no specific reference to the couple, but is irradiated by it. Our response to the Éluardian 'nous' is here, as in 'Couvre-feu', permeated by an awareness that the couple is its lowest common denominator; and the language of the poem's fourth section signals how an amatory vocabulary is able to relocate itself in an ever more generalized utterance:

> Mains par nos mains reconnues
> Lèvres à nos lèvres confondues

This is a kind of utterance in which hands are as much agents of forward momentum, as of physical contact, even though that forward momentum may at times be hindered:

> Avec vos lourdes mains dans l'huile paresseuse
> De vos actes anciens

and in which lips are not merely an erogenous zone, but the point at which the word is made flesh:

> Nous parlerons ensemble un langage sensible

'Sans âge' gathers into itself factors already mentioned elsewhere: the peculiarly penetrative and prelapsarian self-surrender of the child, the connection between processes of self-multiplication and egalitarianism (lines 31–2). It puts before us, too, some previously unencountered notions.

First, we should pick out Éluard's acute sense of scale: in this poem, we meet the phrase 'à ma mesure' (line 29) and elsewhere in the selection occur the phrases 'à l'échelle humaine', 'à l'échelle animale', 'à hauteur d'homme'. Scale, for Éluard, means the angle of vision best adapted to an order of existence (human, animal, vegetable) for that order to be ascribed its true value in the world. 'Sans âge' is, in part, a poem about man's recovery of an anthropocentric world, a world expressly adjusted to the human scale which depends on being conceived and brought about by humans. But this recovery of human scale is not a way of dominating or possessing the world so much as a way of re-incorporating the environment into the flow of human need and human aspiration.

Second, 'Sans âge' allows us to see the nature of the amatory moment, as opposed to the historical:

> Notre espace certain notre air pur est de taille
> A combler le retard creusé par l'habitude
> Nous aborderons tous une mémoire nouvelle

While the moment of historical event threatens to be fracture, disclosure of solitude, the moment of love is the moment of renewal and expansion to inhabit the totality of space. The sequence of *habitual* actions is entropic and attritional, decelerating and thus increasingly lagging behind the actual ('le retard creusé par l'habitude'); the past grows heavier as it recedes and paralyses us (see lines 24–5 already quoted). But the newness of the amatory moment does not destroy continuity; it creates its own continuity:

> Nous aborderons tous une mémoire nouvelle

or, put another way:

> C'est gagner un instant
>   Pour ne plus jamais douter de durer ('Le Baiser', p. 72)

Time's flow becomes indivisible, and past, present and future are gathered into a single moment of full being.

The fertility of the moment is dependent on two related factors. The first is light and the second is infinite visibility:

> Je parle de te voir
> Je te sais vivante
> Tout existe tout est visible
> Il n'y a pas une goutte de nuit dans tes yeux
>
> Je vis dans une lumière exclusive la tienne
>     ('Telle femme, principe de vie, interlocutrice idéale', p. 70)

Out of the night of solitude, of dreams that do not have the same free-ranging ease as actuality, springs the light, the light which is a pledge of innocence recovered, in whose play everything cannot but be affirmed – shadow itself may be an affirmation of the lighted figure – in which everything can traffic with everything else. Light is a necessary condition of the face-to-face relationship between lovers, in which all other relationships are conceived and from which all knowledge flows. Éluard's sunlit world is a world of looks ('regards'); looks are the essential currency, more fundamental even than words. And these looks are infinitely self-begetting:

> Belles clés des regards clés filles d'elles-mêmes ('L'Extase', p. 78)

The look's continual self-regeneration depends on the mirror, on processes of reflection, reflections on which the onlooker relies both to see himself and to *see*:

> Qui me reflète sinon toi moi-même je me vois si peu
> Sans toi je ne vois rien qu'une étendue déserte
> Entre autrefois et aujourd'hui          ('Je t'aime', p. 86)

And these reflections are diversified by all kinds of reflective mechanisms, diffusion, deflection, distortion (in a non-pejorative sense) – looks criss-crossing in space, reflections bouncing back or dispersing. Occasionally the space thus traversed by the eyes remains resolutely empty; the surface of the mirror is transparent, opening up on to nothing (here 'miroir' becomes 'vitre'), and space itself is imaged as the deserted square (see 'Giorgio de Chirico', p. 87). But usually looks are fruitfully exchanged and act out the couple's ways of relating: mutuality, reciprocity, complementarity. And those ways of relating radiate from the centre, which the couple is, through all visible things, which, in their turn, relate in those same ways, both with each other and with the poet. So it is that the love of the couple reverberates beyond the couple and becomes the principle inspiring the poet's perception of reality; the poet, contemplating the loved one, can conjure her up only through the analogies and associations which her figure suggests; she is, in fact, the very force of analogy itself.

Love, in Éluard's poetry, is thus a *direction*, the projection of creative desire beyond the desire to possess. The loved one is not so much a goal of enjoyment, as the beginning of all sentient possibilities and the promise of continual meta- morphosis and creative change. Éluard is fond of quoting these lines from Baudelaire's dedication to *Les Paradis artificiels*:

> La femme est l'être qui projette la plus grande ombre ou la plus grande lumière dans nos rêves. La femme est fatalement suggestive; elle vit d'une autre vie que la sienne propre; elle vit spirituellement dans les imaginations qu'elle hante et qu'elle féconde.

The loved one is the image of all images, most alive, perhaps, in the imaginative fertility she begets. Is this, then, to say that love is a force whose significance far exceeds those who embody it? Certainly this is what Éluard's words on de Sade imply:

> il a voulu délivrer l'imagination amoureuse de ses propres objets. Il a cru que de là, et de là seulement, naîtrait la véritable égalité.

The amorous imagination, freed from the limitations of any specific realization, not constrained by any acquisitive designs, is able freely to explore the field of its own energies. Love is neither given nor taken, nor indeed shared, but rather shared *in*; love is generated by lovers not so much for their own private pleasure as to open up a space of exhilaration, of common illumination, where all perception is intensified.

But possessive love is something which has to be unlearned. Although Éluard had already arrived at the collective 'nous' in *Le Devoir et l'inquiétude*, this 'nous' was still a particular group bound together by a common wartime experience and was separate from the domestic, self-regarding couple of *Poèmes pour la paix*. And many of the poems which have Gala as their inspiration, poems up to 1928, are marked by the sense of love as a solitary struggle – a struggle of the lover with himself and of the lover with the loved one. It is out of the relationship with Nusch that the love of the couple emerges as an act of intercession on behalf of mankind. This view of love as mediation, as the ground of all fellow feeling, underpins the poems of the Second World War, and survives even the profound despair and the temporary refusal to imagine a future, occasioned by Nusch's sudden death. The final poem of *Le Temps déborde*, 'Notre vie [2]', mocks the solitary, and the Gothic fairy tale he insists on living in:

> Nous n'irons pas au but un par un mais par deux
> Nous connaissant par deux nous nous connaîtrons tous
> Nous nous aimerons tous et nos enfants riront
> De la légende noire où pleure un solitaire

The poetry of love presents its own peculiar collection of linguistic problems. The arts of language are the arts of seduction, of the word made irresistible; and yet the language of love, when it does not serve seduction, is a language of embarrassment, of inarticulacy or of clichés, however deeply felt. In love, we find at once our common condition and a belief in our uniqueness, a uniqueness either strong enough to express itself silently or inventive enough to outleap the cliché (which it cannot really escape) in all manner of decorative elaboration, conceit and fantasy; the language of amorous tribute, in protesting love, expresses an exasperation with language. There is no doubt that, from time to time, Éluard's tributary poetry will strike us as a kind of courtship display and come perilously close to the exhibitionist and meretricious. Generally, however, Éluard's words are so fluid, the concrete and abstract tilt so easily into each other, that no gift-wrapped love-offering results: the poet may start from an utterance that looks merely gallant, but he becomes increasingly absorbed in the play of his own linguistic productivity, so that the loved one is superseded by love itself, as adventure of the imagination. We can perhaps see something of this process in 'La courbe de tes yeux' (p. 65) (see Appendix III). The amorous tribute becomes a poem of immersion in the new sensations revealed by the loved one's eyes. From innocence to daylight, from daylight to visibility, from visibility to vision, such are the steps in the lover's progress. To be seen by the loved one's eyes is also to see with them.

## PICTORIAL

Éluard's connections with contemporary artists were too manifold to allow more than a brief acount of them here. His work was, at one time or another, illustrated by such artists as Valentine Hugo, Magritte, Masson, Miró, André Beaudin, Roger Chastel, Man Ray, Picasso and Jacques Villon; and he engaged in more properly collaborative ventures, particularly with Max Ernst (*Répétitions*, 1922; *Les Malheurs des immortels*, 1922). He wrote poems on a wide variety of artists and he, in his turn, 'illustrated' with poems the drawings and etchings of his friends – *Les Mains libres*, 1937 (drawings by Man Ray); *A l'intérieur de la vue: 8 poèmes visibles*, 1948 (drawings by Max Ernst); *Perspectives*, 1948 (etchings by Albert Flocon). He also collected art-theoretical writings (for example, *Anthologie des écrits sur l'art*, 1952–4).

The close collaboration of the arts in Surrealism was no

accident: writing and picture-making seemed equally available to automatic and associative processes, and one of the more characteristic of Surrealist art-forms, the collage, encouraged different media to give each other access to another way of meaning and another field of reference. Inasmuch as Surrealism wished to privilege a state of mind, a certain utilization of one's unconscious resources, rather than any particular artistic style, so it refused to acknowledge either generical distinctions or the idea that the reader's/spectator's response to a work was generically conditioned. As we look at a Surrealist painting, for example, we may feel that it does not ask us to respond to its pictorial values so much as seduce our imagination; it is not a painted picture, but an image of incitement.

When Éluard comes to write about painters, he is thus not writing an interpretation (critique) nor a *transposition d'art*,[5] nor is he treating painting as a convenient source of images which can be recycled:

> Pour collaborer, peintres et poètes se veulent libres. La dépendance abaisse, empêche de comprendre, d'aimer. Il n'y a pas de modèle pour qui cherche ce qu'il n'a jamais vu. À la fin, rien n'est aussi beau qu'une ressemblance involontaire (*Donner à voir*, 1939)

When Éluard writes a poem on a painter, he is summoning a relationship of osmosis, which allows him to absorb someone else's field of experience. And this reflects the very process of looking at pictures: it is not a matter of intellectual confrontation, where demands are made, values sought and so on, but a gradual assimilation of one mentality by another. In this way, one artist seeks a renewal of his own vision through another; and the difference of medium is not an obstruction, but none the less some safeguard of artistic independence.

Étienne Souriau[6] is right when he describes Surrealist poems on painters as efforts to share the imagining mechanisms of someone else; but his description of Éluard's poem

'A Marc Chagall' as a 'poème à la manière de Marc Chagall' (p. 44) still suggests too transpositional an undertaking, as though Éluard were making a journey *into* Chagall, rather than *with* him through similar territory. Roger Chastel's account of the relationship between his drawings and the poems of Éluard's *Bestiaire*, on the other hand, is a perfect definition of Surrealist 'illustration', where looking at a picture or reading a text are already forms of illustration:

> Les courbes du dessin épousent les inflexions du mot, le verbe se continue dans le trait, *on n'illustre pas un livre on le prolonge ... dans un autre domaine sensible.*

Reading, spectation, illustration have a new meaning: they are not acts of paraphrase and decipherment, but acts of modulation into a different perceptual mode and of correlation. Some consideration of Éluard's poem on Giorgio de Chirico (p. 87) may clarify this distinction.

De Chirico's pictures of city squares of 1913–17 (such as *The Joys and Enigmas of a Strange Hour*, 1913; *The Anguish of Departure*, 1914; *The Enigma of a Day*, 1914) use an unrelenting linearity and severe classical perspective to create an almost vertiginous illusion of deep space, into which the eye is sucked, across empty ground, past arcaded buildings and impassive, authoritarian statues. These squares and urban spaces are centres of ambiguity; they are ambiguous because they blend the dynamism of the eye with the immobility of their architecture, the penetrability of space (vista, arcade) with elements of impenetrability and blockage (blank windows, closed boxes or vans, walls); this combination of freedom to move and sense of restriction is also expressed, more obliquely, in the depiction of figures with space at their disposal, but surrounded by images of authority (public statues, classical architecture). Sometimes de Chirico resorts to contradictory perspectives, so that planes tilt against each other and arcades twist around on themselves and become labyrinthine (for example, *The Anxious Voyage*, 1913). The atmosphere is equally ambiguous: a pervasive listlessness is shot through with an inexplicable sense of anxiety and foreboding – the eerie luminosity of the pictures has much to do with this, for shadows are cast by a light whose source is not guaranteed and whose transparency creates a strange airlessness. The geometry of trapezium, triangle, and rectangle, transforms the physicality of architecture into the metaphysicality of shadow and linear configuration. This geometry reveals or imposes the patterns in chance, the inevitability of certain incongruities. De Chirico's paintings present us with infinitely recessive space and infinitely recessive enigmas, walls behind walls, arcades within arcades, rooms behind windows.

It will already be evident at how many points Éluard's poem meets the de Chirican landscape. His, too, is a landscape in which light is hauntingly divorced from its source:

> La lumière en relief
> Sur le ciel qui n'est plus le miroir du soleil

in which walls give way to other walls, circles operate within circles (lines 3–4), shadows created by light flee from it (line 2). If de Chirico's world is ambiguously suspended between polarities, the values of Éluard's world are constantly subject to inversion: where previously light had been a source of protection, this function is now assumed by the shadow; the place of the 'maîtres' (line 10) is taken over by their former slave ('je'). And then there are the specific ambiguities of the genderless 'tour' (tower, trick, trip), of 'défendre' (protection and prohibition) and of 'autour' (positional and dynamic). And de Chirico's motifs of statues, city squares, shadows, blocked trains, are to be found elsewhere in Éluard's poetry.

But the poem is not merely an imitation; it is the point of confluence of two imaginations, tapping resources in its own, poetic, medium, such as Lamartine's 'L'Isolement': 'Un seul être vous manque et tout est dépeuplé'. And Lori Walters[7] picks out other, less obvious, but equally suggestive, lines and phrases in Lamartine's poem – 'Je contemple la terre, ainsi qu'une ombre errante', 'un ciel sombre ou pur', 'Mes yeux verraient partout le vide et les déserts', 'la terre d'exil' – which relate to other springs in Éluard's own experience. For this is, after all, a love-poem, difficult to interpret perhaps, but indicating the poet's exclusion from a world, the world of the loved one apparently, which he is too dependent on to be able to erase ('dépeupler'). Caught in a state of limbo, the poet remembers a time when the full light of the sky was protection enough for the confident being; but now the reflective capacity of the sky has been usurped by the walls which reflect his silence, and the self-annihilation sought in the shadow is unachievable for the individual who knows too well that he is powerless and banished.

The silence, ghostly light and deep space, created by the elongated shadows, dramatic perspective and diminished figures, which are characteristic of de Chirico's canvases, have left unmistakable traces in the work of Tanguy, Magritte, Delvaux and Dali. This redemption of classical perspective by many Surrealists is of some significance. For one thing, perspective plunges us towards the horizon of the perceptible and beckons us beyond; for another, given that perspective is a conventional, 'rational' way of ordering space, the Surrealists were able to use this convention to outrage conventionality, to use the very tools of reason in order to alienate reason and engage the spectator in the cognition of what is beyond comprehension.

Perspective also provides a convenient model of Éluard's imagination. In his thoughts on perspective published in the journal *Derrière le miroir* in 1948, Albert Flocon, a set of whose etchings Éluard 'illustrated' with poems (*Perspectives*, 1948), has this to say of the vanishing point:

> Le point de fuite contient toutes choses en puissance, car toute chose vue d'assez loin s'y réduit. Point de mire et feu central, il envoie ses rayons partout et les reçoit de toutes parts.

Flocon's vanishing point has much in common with the

Éluardian mirror, so often represented by the loved one. The mirror has the power to draw all phenomena into its frame; distance itself collapses into the single plane of the mirror's surface. And moreover, it is a centre of radiation, of the endless generation of images. The vanishing point is, furthermore, a means of reconciling the parallel and the convergent; Flocon describes this capacity thus:

> Les parallèles sont censées ne jamais se rencontrer, sauf dans l'infini. Or en perspective elles se rencontrent dans le point de fuite. Elles forment les rayons d'un cercle et sont pourtant parallèles. Les centres où tendent ces rayons sont magnétisés, ils entraînent puissamment notre fantaisie.

Éluard's vision is one that ever seeks connections and fusions while not wishing to undo our sense of the different kinds of reality which run parallel and slip against each other – the relationship between the human and animal worlds is a case in point.

And Éluard's versification might itself be linked helpfully with these notions of perspective: the high degree of regularity in Éluard's versification acts, like perspective, as a stabilizing point of reference which, paradoxically, gives leverage to the unstable, and the incongruous; set in the context of the recognized, the unrecognized both pleads recognizability and *defines* its distance from the recognizable.

But the rigorously measured space of perspective is by no means the only kind of space which aptly exemplifies or inspires Éluard's vision. The 'soft' space of another variety of psychic experience, to be found in the work of Marc Chagall, is an equally potent model. Chagall's space is peculiarly yielding and peculiarly palpable, an almost amniotic substance in which the recurrent ingredients of his imagination – the ass, the cow, the violin/ist, the cockerel, the clock, the loving couple – float or rest, free of gravity. And these recurrent motifs have no fixed values: we come to accept their inescapability as psychic indices, but their relationships with each other shift through all combinations and equations.

Éluard re-established contact with Chagall on the latter's return to France from the USA after the war, in 1946, and out of this contact grew *Le Dur Désir de durer* (1946), a collection of nineteen poems, illustrated with twenty-five drawings and a coloured frontispiece by Chagall and dedicated to him. In 'A Marc Chagall' (p. 94), Éluard searches out the affinities between his vision and that of the painter, in three four-line stanzas, three points of view woven round the loving couple, who occupy and create their own space (see Appendix III).

Notions of visibility are central to Éluard's way of thinking about poetry:

> Voir, c'est comprendre, juger, transformer, imaginer,
>     oublier ou s'oublier, être ou disparaître.
> Voir, c'est recevoir, refléter c'est donner à voir.
> Le poète *voit* dans la même mesure qu'il *se montre*. Et
>     réciproquement.                    (*Donner à voir*, 1939)

We have already examined the significance of eye, look and reflection for the lover: love itself is an achievement of seeing; the eyes make sensory contact a prerequisite of knowledge. But there is another sense in which one could call Éluard's poetry visible. Language tends towards the definitional, the analytic, the purposive; it is a mode of address and is, thus, by nature, vocative. The picture, on the other hand, is mute and accusative; it bears witness, it is an offering of evidence. Pictures do not in themselves provide a medium of discourse; in other words, they do not have structures for intellectual systematization in the same way as the written word, and this makes the comprehension of pictures a process which it is difficult to know how to perform. This is why picture-titles are such crucial factors; they deliver the spectator from the recalcitrant, pure 'thereness' of the image and direct looking towards interpretation. This quality of the visual image is something that Éluard pursues, with the notion of 'l'évidence poétique'. Like the picture, the poem, for all that it may have a first person perspective, offers itself as a document which resists easy intellectual manipulation and enforces intuitive inhabitation. The 'purity' of Éluard's verse lies here, in this kind of guileless enigma.

### ANIMAL

In 1948, Éluard assembled the majority of his animal poems in a single collection, *Le Bestiaire*, with coloured etchings by Roger Chastel. Chastel's illustrations of Colette's *De la patte à l'aile* had given Éluard the idea, but he had long been interested in the bestiary as a genre. This was not only because it exemplified that candid medieval moralism, harvested straight from the people, which coincided so naturally with his own persuasions, but also because it offered the kind of perceptual shift – the world seen 'à l'échelle animale', as an adaptation to the peculiar patterns and needs of animal life – which might regenerate our own engagement with our environment. In a note on the medieval poet Philippe de Thaun, for his *Première anthologie vivante de la poésie du passé* (1951), Éluard refers to Philippe's bestiary (*c*. 1125) thus:

> Son bestiaire, premier du genre dans notre littérature, reprend un héritage antique à travers la tradition populaire, inaugurant ainsi la longue lignée moraliste des poètes et des conteurs qui se servirent d'animaux pour critiquer et enseigner les hommes.

The undertaking of the bestiarist would seem to be very similar to that of the writer of fables, to allow men to see more clearly into their condition and behaviour by means of a detour through the animal kingdom. Why, then, does Éluard omit La Fontaine from his anthology? Because La Fontaine's treatment of the animal world is too exploitative, too cynical, too limited to an apology for the rights of the strongest; he is a prisoner of his pursuit of the *aptness* of the animal/human parallel; and thus he denies himself the opportunity of renewing his perception of the human world by yielding the initiative to the mysteries of the inalienably animal.

The fundamental difference between the bestiarist and the fabulist is that the one deals in images (or emblems), the other in actions; the one in the instantaneous energies of something 'seen', the other in dramatized argument resolving itself into proverbial maxim. And so the bestiarist surprises moral implications in what innocently caught his imagination, while the fabulist has his end in view from the start and funnels his narrative towards its lesson. For Éluard, the emphasis in his animal poems is on 'enseigner' rather than 'critiquer', but the teachings of the animals do not have the allegorical thrust of traditional bestiary and fable. They involve adjustments of perception which shift familiar phenomena into another dimension, never far from us, and somehow desired by us; animals become the agents whereby we embed ourselves in existence at more points of our being, whereby we extend our capacity for empathy.

Habits of anthropomorphism are deeply ingrained, language inevitably encourages us to envisage animal actions in human terms; and if the intercourse between the animal and human worlds has been unproblematic, it is largely because an exclusively human reference has controlled it. Similes have compared humans with animals and vice versa, but they have rested on the assumption that animals operate with much the same behavioural codes and emotional capacities as we do. How are our condescensions towards animals to be avoided, how are we to acknowledge the difference of their existence without making them alien?

If we look at Éluard's use of simile in the poems from *Les Animaux et leurs hommes*, ... (1920), we discover what may at first seem to be contradictory tendencies. On the one hand, though a simile may be essentially anthropomorphic, its anthropomorphism does not act in a familiarizing way – quite the reverse:

> Le poisson avance
> Comme un doigt dans un gant ('Poisson', p. 99)

Here the disembodiment of the finger, now endowed with a

peculiar life of its own, makes the finger itself a burrowing animal; conversely, we can no longer view the fish's passage through water as one of unhindered smoothness, but must now perceive it as a frictional movement through an element more enclosingly palpable. Alternatively, the very familiarity and aptness of the image, while absorbing the creature into our world, ensures a reanimation of our world:

> L'araignée,
> Heureuse de son poids,
> Reste immobile
> Comme le plomb du fil à plomb. ('Fuir', p. 101)

The visual distance between the spider hanging on its thread and the lead weight suspended on the plumb-line is no distance at all. But the lead weight, far from merely functioning as some convenient, illustrative parallel, is itself enhanced by the properties of that which it is meant to serve: the lead, too, is happy in the sense of its own density, in its taut stillness.

What emerges from both these examples is the same principle of reciprocity which motivates the loving couple; here again we find the convertibility of the values of one order of existence into the values of another. Elsewhere, Éluard presents this process of conversion as a process, as a step-by-step transubstantiation. In the poem 'Patte' (p. 101), for example, Éluard uses a graphic device to render the gradations of reality which have to be passed through to get from cat to human: the 'cry' of the cat undergoes a process of erosion ('crier', 'crie', 'cri') as it progresses from cat-ritual to something consonant with human feeling. Equally, the meanings generated by the acoustic relatives of the 'i' sound of 'crier' move from notions of self-affirmation and expansiveness ('s'établit', 'libre') to dejection ('triste'), as the border between one set of expressive possibilities and another is crossed.

It is in his dealings with domestic pets that man is most likely to stifle animal impulses. 'D'une bête' (p. 106) is unashamedly anecdotal. During a stay at Golfe-Juan in the summer of 1951, with Picasso not far away at Vallauris, the bitch belonging to Éluard and Dominique went mad and had to be put down. Here it is the syntax and tone which safeguard the bitch from condescension and the poem from sentimentality (see Appendix III).

### TYPOGRAPHIC AND PROSODIC

As we have seen, Éluard practises continual vigilance in his fight against the poeticization of his own poetry. For all their formal and sacramental qualities, his poems remain exploratory, and open to the contingent, the improvised, the suddenly revealed. Although they may be occasional, the occasion is not the consistent point of reference, but the impetus for a poem that seeks its real centre in a process of constant self-adaptation and self-correction:

> Le poète est dirigé. Il ne fait pas ce qu'il veut, mais ce qu'il peut. Les circonstances s'imposent à lui d'une manière imprévisible. Il veut parler de la femme qu'il aime, il parle des oiseaux; il veut parler de la guerre, il parle de l'amour. Aussi le poète ne connaît le titre de son poème qu'après l'avoir écrit. ('Aujourd'hui la poésie...', extracts from a lecture, 1946)

It is not possible to read a poem of Éluard's as though it were some kind of consecutive discourse; the Éluardian poem is, rather, a sequence of enunciations or notations, the area of visibility, in and through which the mind circulates. There is no anguish in this process of inquiry, and the surprises of the text do not alienate, but liberate, the imagination of the reader. This ease which we have with the text is partly the fluency of our circulation through it, and this fluency, in turn, depends to a considerable extent on the absence of punctuation. *Capitale de la douleur* (1926) is the last properly punctuated verse-collection. Thereafter, from *L'Amour la poésie* (1929) onwards, Éluard's poetry is unpunctuated, apart from terminal full stops, themselves temporarily absent in *Ralentir travaux* (1930) (written in collaboration with Breton and Char).[8]

Inasmuch as punctuation reinforces syntactic and semantic hierarchies and, by means of pauses, signals the presence of time in the text, so its omission allows all the parts of the text to assume equal importance, and also helps to make them simultaneous with each other in a time of their own. Furthermore, the omission of punctuation obscures grammatical connections: in Éluard's characteristically nominal constructions, we are often likely to be uncertain whether juxtaposed nouns stand in an enumerative or appositional relationship to each other, and in the following line:

> Mon corps vivant charmant ma raison ma déraison
> ('Vivante et morte séparée', p. 82)

the problem created by the string of nouns is exacerbated by our doubts about whether 'vivant' and 'charmant' are adjectives or present participles.

But it is perhaps the visual effect of the unpunctuated verse which should be insisted upon, for it seems to give the words a peculiar naïveté, a vividness, which bespeaks more a confidence in *them* than in their ability to transmit a particular message. The Éluardian poem exists in an uncluttered space, through which our eyes move, visually feeling the words perhaps more than reading them, acquiring knowledge of them rather than deciphering them.

Éluard's verse never strays far from the sanctions of poetic tradition:

> Tout se passe comme si la poésie libre d'Éluard était brodée sur un canevas de poésie régulière, dont le dessin lui sert toujours de guide, de point de départ ou de point d'appui. (Jean Mazaleyrat, p. 28  see Select Bibliography)

But this is hardly surprising. It is important that however elusive or obscurely intuited his meanings may be, we should be able to inhabit a world which is largely familiar. It is important, too, that we should feel beneath the processes of metamorphosis, rupture and juxtaposition, supporting patterns of equilibrium and ordering, of communal availability. Éluard finds that poetic machinery which permits the constant publicization of the intimate and densely subjective, and pursues a path between what is self-generating and what is ordained: 'L'Extase' (p. 78), a poem written four days before Nusch's death, provides a good example (see Appendix III).

Éluard does, of course, take liberties with the rules of poetry, but these liberties are more or less restricted to heterometricity, rare instances of syncope (the elision of an 'e' within a word), more frequent instances of apocope (the elision of an 'e' at the end of a word) and a disregarding of rhyme. Apocope in Éluard's work is not so much breaking with tradition as re-establishing links that go further back. We find a line with an apocope at the caesura (or *césure épique*)[9] in 'L'Extase':

Où des miroirs s'embu(ent) où des miroirs s'éclairent
(4+2+4+2)

and we find another at the end of 'D'une bête' (p. 106):

Sur notre chienne absent(e) notre chienne exigeante
(4+2+3+3)

The first line of 'Ta chevelure d'oranges' (p. 64) contains two apocopes (one a *césure épique*):

Ta chevelur(e) d'orang(es) dans le vide du monde
(4+2+3+3)
Dans le vide des vitres lourdes de silence (3 + 3 + 2 + 4)

But why after all, is not this first line a line of fourteen syllables, giving the rhythmic pattern 4 + 3 + 4 + 3? Certainly there is no principle that compels us to practise the apocopes in our reading; the compulsion, if compulsion there is, lies in our desire to find a way back to a familiar

four-measure alexandrine and to make the first three lines
share a certain rhythmic consistency. The truth is, however,
that this first line is rhythmically ambiguous. We can argue
that it is necessary to count all the 'e's in order to underline
the persistence of their hypnotic undertone through the first
two lines and to make evident the repetitive structure – 3 'e's
per line:

> Ta chevelur*e* d'orang*es* dans le vid*e* du monde
> Dans le vid*e* des vitr*es* lourd*es* de silence

Equally it may be argued that the 'e's of 'vide', 'vitres'
'lourdes' are intended as *empty* self-dissipating reverbations
and that the 'e's of 'chevelure' and 'oranges' should accord-
ingly be dropped to emphasize, by contrast, their compact
plenitude. At all events, we should recognize that Éluard's
freer handling of the terminal 'e' introduces a degree of
rhythmic elasticity into many of his lines which contributes to
their fluidity and the elusiveness of what they express.

Two further areas of rhythmic interest should be men-
tioned. First, we have already seen how crucial the role of
the long line is, not only from consideration of 'L'Extase'
(see Appendix III), but also from brief comments on the first
'Critique de la poésie' (see p. 11): the long line is often a
moment of expansive confidence, or of relaxation into plain
speaking, or enacts the aimless meandering of a consciousness
that has lost its way. But the short line may be equally
conspicuous and the variation of line-length in general an
important expressive resource. Second, given that Éluard's
lines are predominantly parisyllabic (hexasyllables, octo-
syllables, decasyllables, alexandrines), instances of impari-
syllabic lines may be structurally significant. In 'Le front aux
vitres' (p. 66), for example, the two imparisyllabic lines:

> Je te cherche par-delà l'attente        (3 + 4 + 2) (9)
>
> Par-delà moi-même                       (3 + 2) (5)

are a transitional passage between the first five lines, which
are circumscribed by the repeated line:

Le front aux vitres comme font les veilleurs de chagrin

and the two octosyllables which close the poem:

| | |
|---|---|
| Et je ne sais plus tant je t'aime | (5 + 3) |
| Lequel de nous deux est absent | (5 + 3) |

It is in the imparisyllabic lines that the second person is first introduced; in these lines the condition of waiting – the condition that governs the first five lines – and the condition of solitude and self-limitation are transcended. Out of the nervous instability of the imparisyllabic line, and its very aspiration for evenness, emerges the poet's discovery of the totality of his love within himself that makes absence and presence interchangeable; and this is expressed in two, rhythmically equivalent, octosyllables.

The phonetic patterning in Éluard's verse may serve general structural ends or may be evidence of the peculiarly organic and improvised radiation of his text, or both. In 'Poisson' (p. 99), for example, the first and last stanzas are informed by the 'u' (phonetic) common to 'douce', 'bouge', 'pour', 'touche', and the 'or' (phonetic) of 'transforment' is echoed in 'porte' and 'emporte', but in a nicely chiastic arrangement – 'or' precedes 'u' in the first stanza and is part of a verb which describes the action of fish, swimmers and boats on water, while in the last stanza 'u' precedes 'or' which is now part of verbs which describe the action of water on its inhabitants. Furthermore, the collective definite article 'les' has become, by the final stanza, the singular generical 'le', as fish, swimmer, boat, participating more profoundly in their element, participate too in the water's all-synthesizing singleness, 'l'eau'. This change has already begun to occur in the second stanza, though here the particular and single are not yet the generical because of their specified different activities. And this stanza is dominatd by a different tonality, the nasal vowel ā of 'avance', 'dans', 'gant', 'danse', 'lentement', a sound noticeably absent, however, from the final line:

Et la voile respire

Here the slow, hypnotic movements of fish and swimmer and the self-engrossment of the acoustic texture find a channel of release from the water into the air, from one element into another; so the boat, which in one phonetic sense has the closest ties with the water (bateau/eau), is also the instrument by which the liquid communicates with the non-liquid.

In speaking of these clearly structural acoustic patterns, I have purposely avoided assigning to them any expressive value, for two reasons. First, their organizational function can be demonstrated, is not an arbitrary supposition (in the way that the supposition that 'u' sounds suggest, say, coolness, leisure or delicacy is). Second, if sounds do have expressive values, then these will probably be derived, consciously or unconsciously, from the meanings of the words in which the sounds appear. As we read through a sequence of words related by similar sounds, therefore, it is fitting that we should let their meanings contaminate each other, so that we hear softness in 'bouger', or touch in 'douce'; indeed we may be influenced by other acoustically related words which though absent from the poem belong to the poet's characteristic vocabulary – thus, for example, 'douce', 'bouger' perhaps engender in our minds 'couler', 'toujours', 'bouche', 's'ouvre' and so on.

From looking at these assonating groups of words, it is not difficult to see how one can speak of a sequence of words as the passage of a sound or sounds through a process of transformation and growth. In the line from 'Ta chevelure d'oranges' –

Ô soupirs d'ambre, rêves, regards
(o supiʀ dābʀə, ʀɛvə, ʀəgaʀ)

the 'ʀə' sound sets out on a journey of exploration, a journey really begun in the previous line with the word 'ressemble', a journey which includes the modulation of 'ʀə' in 'ʀɛ' ('rêves'). The text seems to generate itself, ad-libbing to its own tune, feeling its way forward through its own desires, its own deep acoustic impulses. Out of the 'soupirs d'ambre', where 'soupir' reflects 'désir' and where 'ambre' is a blend of the nasal vowel of 'oranges' and the consonantal material of 'ombre', are born the space of dream and the fruitfulness of exchanged looks, developments which are woefully short-lived, for the potential infinity of metamorphosis is cut short by a memory of absence.

In our attention to these phonetic patterns, we should not overlook the significant part played by grammatically humbler words. The definite article, so essential to Éluard's poetic enterprise, with its liquid 'l', aptly called the 'friction-less continuant', may, on its own, colour a whole passage, quite apart from its alliterative connections with other words. The alliterative insistence of the various grammatical forms of the second person singular – tu, te, toi, ton, tien – may centre attention on the changing roles, the inexhaustible resourcefulness of the loved one, now motivator of the world, now receiver, now both, now just herself in herself, now magical possessor. Or it may be the preposition 'de' with its voiced plosive which is the key to the burgeoning of the text:

La courbe de tes yeux  fait le tour de mon cœur
Un rond de danse et de douceur    (p. 65)

In the first line, 'de' acts as the pivot of the two two-noun groups, and in the second, moves from this more passive function to a productive one: it triggers 'danse' and 'douceur', as if drawing them out of its own potentialities.

Éluard makes little use of line-terminal rhyme, and when it occurs, it has a structuring rather than structural effectiveness; half-rhyme relationships (assonance and consonance), or repetition, are favoured more by him, and these acoustic echoes pervade the whole verse-texture and are not confined to a position of privilege at the end of the line. This is not to say that Éluard does not occasionally find obtrusive rhyme a useful resource. In the opening lines of 'Chat' (p. 100), for instance:

Pour ne poser qu'un doigt dessus
Le chat est bien trop grosse bête.
    Sa queue rejoint sa tête ...

the rhyme momentarily beckons us towards the nursery-
rhyme or nonsense-poem, and its inbuilt associative mechan-
ism pushes the verse off in a new direction. The rhyme of the
last two lines of 'L'Amoureuse' (p. 64), on the other hand:

> Ses rêves en pleine lumière
> ....
> Me font rire, pleurer et rire,
> Parler sans avoir rien à dire

not only explains the final line by relating it to 'rire' ('parler
sans avoir rien à dire' is, like 'rire', speech important only as
a desire to express – 'rire' = 'rien à dire'), but also resolves
into consciousness and fullness a 'rhyme' structure which has
never properly surfaced, either because of the haphazardness
of the rhyming words ('paupières', 'ouverts', 'lumière';
'dormir') or because relationships are acoustically incomplete
('miens', 'mains'; 'miens', 'ciel'; 'ciel', 'soleil'; 'dormir',
'soleil'). The finding of rhyme coincides with the poet's
discovery of utterance.

Éluard is nevertheless aware of the inevitable focusing
effect of the line-ending. As demonstrated in Appendix III,
the eruption of Gabriel Péri's name is engineered by a
sequence of line-terminal 'i's, and terminal 'i's equally
organize our perception of the loved one's capacities in the
opening lines of 'Tu te lèves...' (p. 73) – 'se déplie',
's'épanouit', 'abîmes', 'racine', 's'établit'. But clearly rhyme
and half-rhyme are, in Éluard, not so much looked for as
discovered, where they lie, as intermittent emergences, from
utterance, of harmony, reflection, echo. We are not likely to
find rhymes consolidated in particular areas, so much as
scattered almost haphazardly through the length of the poem.
In this way they are all but effaced by intervening lines, and
operate in our minds subliminally, inconspicuously drawing
the poem into larger articulations. Thus at one and the same
time the poem is an unpredictable growth and a concerted
falling into place; while lines can enjoy their independence
and have a freedom to enter worlds distant from the preceding

line, so equally they serve a design that only gradually makes itself understood.

## LEXICAL AND SYNTACTIC

As an approach to the Éluardian image, two passages may be juxtaposed: first, an image from Lautréamont's *Les Chants de Maldoror* (1868–9), much cited by Surrealists:

Beau comme la rencontre fortuite sur une table de dissection d'une machine à coudre et d'un parapluie

and second, Pierre Reverdy's observations about the image, quoted by Breton in his first *Manifeste du surréalisme* (1924):

L'image est une création pure de l'esprit.
Elle ne peut naître d'une comparaison mais du rapprochement de deux réalités plus ou moins éloignées.

Plus les rapports des deux réalités rapprochées seront lointains et justes, plus l'image sera forte – plus elle aura de puissance émotive et de réalité poétique....

Reverdy's words seem to favour 'rapprochement' as against 'comparaison', juxtaposition (contiguity) as against explicit simile. One might expect Surrealism to go in scorn of simile: the 'like' of simile signals simile's rational basis and its appeal to *common* knowledge; simile is a comparison intentionally thought up for the occasion and thus strikes us as provisional, even optional, and its function as illustrative; and, besides, there is something powerfully redundant about comparing phenomena already similar. But we should recognize that simile does have a central part to play in Surrealist and Éluardian poetics, for three reasons.

First, the provisional nature of simile suits it to a being-as-becoming, being-as-relation approach – a continuum of ever re-angled views:

J'aspire à ton néant je voudrais voir mon front
Comme un caillou loin dans la terre
Comme un bateau fondu dans l'eau
('Vivante et morte séparée', p. 82)

In his attempt to occupy a nothingness as great and profound as that of the dead Nusch, the poet imagines himself as an inanimate object absorbed into matter; but the pebble, however deeply buried, hangs on to an identity; the boat is more fully effaced, more functionless, and yet is enveloped in a more mobile and animate medium. The poet's project is thus frustrated. Neither of the images is more 'accurate' than the other, each creates the conditions of its own truth while remaining open to qualification by the other, so that the imagination does not treat the images as isolated incidents, but locates its activity in a shifting back and forth between them. As Éluard himself puts it:

> Les rapports entre les choses, à peine établis, s'effacent pour en laisser intervenir d'autres, aussi fugitifs (*Donner à voir*, 1939)

Second, the fact that simile proclaims its rationality and exhibits a demonstrable likeness, makes it more suitable to undermine rationality and demonstrability. Like perspective, simile advertises itself as an exercise in orientation and comprehension. But this ostensibly reasonable figure of speech explodes in our face, not necessarily by confronting us with the total arbitrariness of the 'comme' – as in the Lautréamont example – but by offering to our critical judgement motions of the mind which are hopelessly out of judgement's reach.

Third, simile is voice-derived in a way that metaphor is not. In simile, the poet explicitly enters the creative process and *utters* images, accepts his role as poet. Metaphor, on the other hand, presents itself as something given, having its source not in the poet's embroidering utterance, but in a realm of truth beyond all control and manipulation. The presence of a guiding voice-tone in Éluard's poetry has already been referred to (see p. 7) and simile is one of the ways that tone enters the poem.

Metaphor, however, seems to be more to the Surrealist's purpose. Metaphor is not a comparison, but an identification – not X is *like* Y, but X *is* Y – and thus is essentialist rather than relative, revealed rather than invented, demanding commitment and unavailable to judgement. Where the 'like' of simile makes us aware of a writer's presence, metaphor seems to issue from sources beyond the poet. Metaphor is easily imaginable as an eruption of the irrational unconscious or as a linguistic manifestation of 'le hasard objectif', an identification of one phenomenon with another which has all the look of chance and all the force of inevitability, a projection of desire:

> Dans les coques de glaises on a semé des corbeaux
> Aux ailes fanées au bec de tremblement de terre
> ('Une pour toutes', p. 68)

The identification, here, of crows' beaks with earthquake brooks no objections. Faced with the threat of being taken beyond the comprehensible, we find ways of 'defusing' metaphor: first, we label it a 'figure of speech' and thus make it part of literature's *accepted* arsenal of effects, and then we treat metaphor as though it were simile, making transformations and substitutions until a point of similarity can be found. Thus in the example, we might concentrate on the beak as an organ of sound, on the crow's grating, rasping cry, and find in that sound the sound of falling masonry; or we might think of the crow as a bird of ill-omen, its beak the organ of oracular and fatal judgement, foretelling the apocalypse of earthquake. But this is to misuse metaphor, which is a *total* identification, not a parallelling of selected items. And besides these rationalizing processes are precisely what Surrealism abhors; metaphor can only maintain its primitive and creational power if it is envisaged literally – as a matter of at least imaginary fact, as a radical reorganization of our world, or of our perception of it.

Metaphor is implied in Lautréamont's simile (the sewing-machine and umbrella are on a dissecting table and thus to be identified with a corpse or parts of a corpse) but to think in this way is not so fruitful a strategy as to treat the triad – sewing-machine, umbrella and dissecting table – as a juxtaposition, a relationship of 'rapprochement'. Such a strategy leaves metaphor and simile available as modes of connection, while inviting all other varieties of affiliation. Unlike metaphor and simile, juxtaposition does not differentiate between a base-utterance and what is imaged on that base. Thus no greater credibility is given to any particular element, and no presuppositions about what is literal and what is figurative are made. Consequently, too, the text is governed by an egalitarian principle: nothing exists at the expense of anything else, every item can play its full part in the construction of the poem's alternative reality. And the enumerative structure of much of Éluard's poetry is itself a guarantee of that egalitarian principle.

Some of the features of Éluard's syntax have already been examined, and Appendix III has an analysis of the important role played by the article and the way in which genitive constructions complicate and intensify his appositional sequences in 'La courbe de tes yeux'. Reference has also been made to Éluard's promotion of the child as a model of consciousness. One critic at least, Georges Jean,[10] suggests that Éluard's poetry is, in its very structure, imbued with the spirit of the child: it has a childlike forthrightness in its reliance on nouns, in its imperative nature, in its relative lack of adjectives, in its frequent use of the simple copula ('être'), in its ellipses and overriding presentness. As for the child, so for Éluard, to speak is to bring into existence.

Éluard's syntax is predominantly paratactic, that is to say, it is a syntax built on sequences of discrete clauses without conjunctive connections (apart from coordinating conjunctions), in short, a syntax of juxtaposition:

Tu te lèves l'eau se déplie
Tu te couches l'eau s'épanouit

Tu es l'eau détournée de ses abîmes
Tu es la terre qui prend racine
Et sur laquelle tout s'établit ('Tu te lèves...', p. 73)

Such a syntax presents us with a world both peculiarly patent and peculiarly mysterious. Looked at from one point of view, parataxis is another manifestation of the poet's *disponibilité*, of the permeability of his verse to different sensations, to different modes of experience, and the interpenetration of these different sensations and modes of experience is so natural a process that no conjunctive explanation is required. From another point of view, the lack of conjunctions conceals or erases causality and dependence; we see chains of effects only, produced by an impenetrable magic, whose laws relate to no known system, apart from the system generated by the poem.

And this syntax is further characterized by a preponderance of nouns and scarcity of adjectives. But the preponderance of nouns does not mean that Éluard's poetic world is a highly physical one: as we have seen, Éluard's concrete nouns constantly traffic with the abstract or are made elusive by their generical nature; Éluard's poetic vision may be of the visible, but the reader often has difficulty in visualizing what is put before his eyes. The scarcity of adjectives has much, I am sure, to do with two considerations. The first is the poet's desire to empty his poetry, as far as possible, of personality and opinion, to avoid that kind of intrusion – the attribution of values – which prejudices the activity of the poetic text in the reader's mind. The second and related consideration is to ensure that the noun achieves its qualities, not simply by having them bestowed by adjectives, but through its dynamism within the text, through the various kinships it forms with other words in the poem. The former of these hypotheses would lead one to expect an increased presence of adjectives in Éluard's more polemical verse, the verse of political commitment, for example, where rhetorical effectiveness depends on some injection of emotional or evaluative colouring.

Éluard's poem on 'Gabriel Péri' (p. 59) will remind us that he looks upon words as peculiarly powerful instruments:

Il y a des mots qui font vivre

There is no doubt that, on occasion, words can delude us, lead us into hypocrisies ('Critique de la poésie', p. 53) or threaten to satisfy us with substitute existences. But these are only temporary fallings from grace. The word, when given its independence and allowed to capitalize upon its own dormant energies, will discover and develop its affinities with other words, will find its appointed place in a whole system of words. And in so doing, it will lead what it signifies into an existence which is both integrated and protean. When, in the entry for 'Langage' in the *Dictionnaire abrégé du surréalisme* (1938), Éluard writes:

> Il nous faut peu de mots pour exprimer l'essentiel, il nous faut tous les mots pour le rendre réel.... Les mots gagnent.

he is differentiating between words which merely express ('exprimer') reality and words which form one body with it ('le rendre réel'). Words, for Éluard, are tantamount to a revelation of the laws of life; and words, like life, should be envisaged as never less than a totality, as an infinite play of reflection and reciprocity, as a continuous process of growth and change. The conquest of words, of words not in our vocabulary or of the mysteries which persist in familiar words, is an extension of our living space, more territory won back from silence and solitude. This is a theme to which Éluard returns, but it is never more clearly expressed than in *Quelques-uns des mots qui jusqu'ici m'étaient mystérieusement interdits* (1937), which exploits variations in typography (designed by Guy Levis Mano) to invest words with a visible strangeness. The poem ends with the lines:

Ô mon empire d'homme
Mots que j'écris ici
Contre toute évidence
Avec le grand souci
De tout dire.

Words are the evidence against the evidence of loss, negation and incompleteness. Every man's empire is the cosmos of his own lexicon, with which everything can be said.

# NOTES TO THE INTRODUCTION

1 Picabia was not a member of the *Littérature* group but had started his own Dadaist journal, *391*, in Barcelona in 1917.
2 'Words-in-freedom' are part of Marinetti's programme for a revolution in poetry (1913), involving the destruction of syntax, condensed metaphors and telegraphic images, the absence of punctuation and all typographical restraints, and the exploitation of onomatopoeia. 'Noise-sound' derives from Luigi Russolo's *Art of Noises* (1913), which calls for the abandonment of the limited, worn-out music of instruments in favour of the variegated harmonies of those noises by which we are surrounded in the modern city (hiss, crash, crackle, roar, and so on).
3 For another view, see András Vajda, 'Dada dans la poésie d'Éluard', *Europe*, no. 525, January 1973, pp. 231–42.
4 I adapt here words spoken by Éluard in Moscow, at the 150th anniversary of Hugo's birth, in an address entitled 'Hugo, poète vulgaire': 'Bien sûr que son amour de la nature et de l'homme et que sa sensibilité et son imagination étaient vulgaires, car il n'était qu'un être collectif qui se nommait Hugo.'
5 Louis Chéronnet, in his review of *Voir* (1948), gives a good definition of *transposition d'art* when he describes Éluard's poetic treatment of painters thus: 'le poète accorde sa longueur d'onde sur celle du peintre, tentant de retransmettre en valeurs "mots" les valeurs plastiques de l'artiste'. But this is a view of Éluard's 'pictorial' poems with which I would beg to differ.
6 Étienne Souriau, *La Poésie française et la peinture*, University of London, Athlone Press, 1966 (Cassal Bequest Lecture, 1965).
7 Lori Walters, ' "Giorgio de Chirico": le poème et le peintre', *Neophilologus*, LXIII (April 1979), pp. 212–19.

8 It should be added that there are a few punctuated poems in *Le temps déborde* (1947) and that the first edition of *Corps mémorable* (1947) was punctuated, although the second edition (1948) was not.

9 The *césure épique* is a practice whereby unelided mute 'e's which terminate words at the caesura (at the end of half-lines) are treated like mute 'e's at the end of full lines (that is, they are not counted as syllables). The adjective 'épique' refers to the fact that this practice was common in the medieval French epic.

10 Georges Jean, 'Éluard et l'enfance', *Europe*, no. 525, January 1973, pp. 132–6.

# SELECT BIBLIOGRAPHY

## 1 BIOGRAPHY

Parrot, Louis and Marcenac, Jean, *Paul Éluard*, Paris, Éditions Seghers, 1969.

Ségalat, Roger-Jean, *Album Éluard*, Paris, Gallimard, 1968.

Valette, Robert D., *Éluard: livre d'identité*, Paris, Claude Tchou, 1967.

See also the 'Chronologie' in Paul Éluard, *Œuvres complètes* (ed. Marcelle Dumas and Lucien Scheler), vol. I, Paris, Gallimard, 1968, pp. lix–lxxv.

## 2 CRITICAL STUDIES

Bowie, Malcolm, 'Paul Éluard', in Cardinal, Roger (ed.), *Sensibility and Creation: Studies in Twentieth-Century French Poetry*, London, Croom Helm, 1977, pp. 149–67.

Debreuille, Jean-Yves, *Éluard ou le pouvoir du mot: propositions pour une lecture*, Paris, Nizet, 1977.

Emmanuel, Pierre, *Le Je universel dans l'œuvre d'Éluard*, Paris, GLM, 1948.

Guyard, Marie-Renée, *Le Vocabulaire politique de Paul Éluard*, Paris, Klincksieck, 1974.

Jean, Raymond, *Paul Éluard par lui-même*, Paris, Éditions du Seuil, 1968.

Jean, Raymond, *La Poétique du désir: Nerval Lautréamont Apollinaire Éluard*, Paris, Éditions du Seuil, 1974.

Kittang, Atle, *D'amour de poésie: essai sur l'univers des métamorphoses dans l'œuvre surréaliste de Paul Éluard*, Paris, Minard, 1969.

Mazaleyrat, Jean, 'La Tradition métrique dans la poésie d'Éluard', in Parent, Monique (ed.), *Le Vers français au 20<sup>e</sup> siècle*, Paris, Klincksieck, 1967, pp. 25–42.

Meschonnic, Henri, 'Un langage-solitude. Les formes-sens de "La Vie immédiate" d'Éluard', *Pour la poétique III*, Paris, Gallimard, 1973, pp. 181–274.

Meuraud, Maryvonne, *L'Image végétale dans la poésie d'Éluard*, Paris, Minard, 1966.

Mingelgrün, Albert, 'Essai sur l'évolution esthétique de Paul Éluard: peinture et langage', *L'Information Littéraire*, XXVII (May-June 1975), pp. 116–20.

Picon, Gaëtan, 'Tradition et découverte chez Paul Éluard', *L'Usage de la lecture*, vol. I, Paris, Mercure de France, 1960, pp. 89–104.

Poulet, Georges, 'Éluard', *Études sur le temps humain III: Le Point de départ*, Paris, Plon, 1964, pp. 128–60.

Richard, Jean-Pierre, 'Paul Éluard', *Onze études sur la poésie moderne*, Paris, Éditions du Seuil, 1964, pp. 105–39.

York, R.A., 'Éluard's Game of Construction', *Orbis Litterarum*, XXXII (no. 1, 1977), pp. 83–96.

See also the special numbers of the journal *Europe* devoted to studies of Éluard: nos. 91–2 (July-August 1953); no. 403 (November 1962); no. 525 (January 1973).

3 ANALYSES

Mounin, Georges, 'Un poème d'Éluard ("Couvre-feu")', *La Littérature et ses technocraties*, Paris, Casterman, 1978, pp. 165–71.

Remacle, Madeleine, 'Éluard: "La courbe de tes yeux" ', *Analyses de poèmes français*, Liège, Les Lettres Belges, 1975, pp. 144–52.

Smith, Susan Harris, 'Paul Éluard's "Yves Tanguy", an analysis', *Dada Surrealism*, no. 5, 1975, pp. 49–52.

Wake, C. H., 'Éluard: "L'Extase" ', in Nurse, Peter (ed.), *The Art of Criticism: Essays in French Literary Analysis*, Edinburgh University Press, 1969, pp. 288–99.

Walters, Lori, ' "Giorgio de Chirico": le poème et le peintre', *Neophilologus*, LXIII (April 1979), pp. 212–19.

See also the commentaries on poems by Éluard in Broome, Peter and Chesters, Graham, *The Appreciation of Modern French Poetry 1850–1950* and *An Anthology of Modern French Poetry 1850–1950*, Cambridge University Press, 1976.

# ANTHOLOGIE ÉLUARD

# I
# MORAL AND POLITICAL

1

*Fidèle*

Vivant dans un village calme
D'où la route part longue et dure
Pour un lieu de sang et de larmes
Nous sommes purs.

Les nuits sont chaudes et tranquilles
Et nous gardons aux amoureuses
Cette fidélité précieuse
Entre toutes: l'espoir de vivre.

*J'aime ce poème*

2

Ce n'est pas tous les jours dimanche
Et longue joie... Il faut partir.
La peur de ne pas revenir
Fait que son sort ne change.

Je sais ce qu'il a vu,
Ses enfants à la main,
Gais et si fiers de ce butin,
Dans les maisons et dans les rues.

Il a vu l'endroit où est son bonheur,
Des corsages fleuris d'anneaux et de rondeurs,
Sa femme avec des yeux amusants et troublants,
Comme un frisson d'air après les chaleurs,
Et tout son amour de maître du sang.

3       Le plus tôt en allé
  C'est bien notre douceur et notre pauvreté.

Contents d'avoir trouvé dans la pluie et le vent
  Une tiède maison où boire et reposer
Mes bruyants compagnons ont secoué leur capote
  Et pour rêver ici, plus tard, de ce bonheur
Qui va les prendre pour toujours, ils crient très fort.

Leurs grands gestes font peur au grand froid du dehors.


4       Me souciant d'un ciel dévasté,
      De la pluie qui va nous mouiller
      Je vais pensant au grand bonheur
      Qui nous saisirait si nous voulions.

        Le devoir et l'inquiétude
        Partagent ma vie rude.
        (C'est une grande peine
        De vous l'avouer.)

      Ça sent la verdure à plein nez.
  Sur plein ciel, en plein ciel, le vol des hirondelles
      Nous amuse et nous fait rêver…
      Je rêve d'un espoir tranquille.


5       *Paris si gai!*

    C'est la guerre! Rien n'est plus dur que la guerre
l'hiver!
    Je suis très sale (chez nous on ne marche pas sur le
trottoir, ni dans la rue) mais quelle joie de venir ici se
prélasser!

La ville est toujours ardente. Au cinéma, les gosses sifflent *La Dame aux Camélias*.

Et nous, nous demandons déjà à ceux qui traversent la ville pour aller ailleurs s'ils cherchent des diamants avec une charrue.

6                          *Notre mort*

I

On nous enseigne trop la patience, la prudence – et que nous pouvons mourir.

Mourir, surpris par la plus furtive des lumières, la mort brusque.

«Moi, dans la Belle au bois dormant!» railles-tu, nous faisant rire.

II

> *Je connais tous les chants*
> *des oiseaux.*

Nous avons crié gaiement: «Nous allons à la guerre!» aux gens qui le savaient bien.

Et nous la connaissions!

Oh! le bruit terrible que mène la guerre parmi le monde et autour de nous! Oh! le bruit terrible de la guerre!

Cet obus qui fait la roue,

la mitrailleuse, comme une personne qui bégaie,

et ce rat que tu assommes d'un coup de fusil!

7                          *Novembre 1936*

Regardez travailler les bâtisseurs de ruines
Ils sont riches patients ordonnés noirs et bêtes
Mais ils font de leur mieux pour être seuls sur terre
Ils sont au bord de l'homme et le comblent d'ordures
Ils plient au ras du sol des palais sans cervelle.

*

On s'habitue à tout
Sauf à ces oiseaux de plomb
Sauf à leur haine de ce qui brille
Sauf à leur céder la place.

*

Parlez du ciel le ciel se vide
L'automne nous importe peu
Nos maîtres ont tapé du pied
Nous avons oublié l'automne
Et nous oublierons nos maîtres.

*

Ville en baisse océan fait d'une goutte d'eau sauvée
D'un seul diamant cultivé au grand jour
Madrid ville habituelle à ceux qui ont souffert
De cet épouvantable bien qui nie être en exemple
Qui ont souffert
De la misère indispensable à l'éclat de ce bien.

*

Que la bouche remonte vers sa vérité
Souffle rare sourire comme une chaîne brisée
Que l'homme délivré de son passé absurde
Dresse devant son frère un visage semblable

Et donne à la raison des ailes vagabondes.

8                    *Couvre-feu*

Que voulez-vous la porte était gardée
Que voulez-vous nous étions enfermés
Que voulez-vous la rue était barrée

Que voulez-vous la ville était matée
Que voulez-vous elle était affamée
Que voulez-vous nous étions désarmés
Que voulez-vous la nuit était tombée
Que voulez-vous nous nous sommes aimés.


9                    *Critique de la poésie*

Le feu réveille la forêt
Les troncs les cœurs les mains les feuilles
Le bonheur en un seul bouquet
Confus léger fondant sucré
C'est toute une forêt d'amis
Qui s'assemble aux fontaines vertes
Du bon soleil du bois flambant

García Lorca a été mis à mort

Maison d'une seule parole
Et des lèvres unies pour vivre
Un tout petit enfant sans larmes
Dans ses prunelles d'eau perdue
La lumière de l'avenir
Goutte à goutte elle comble l'homme
Jusqu'aux paupières transparentes

Saint-Pol-Roux a été mis à mort
Sa fille a été suppliciée

Ville glacée d'angles semblables
Où je rêve de fruits en fleur
Du ciel entier et de la terre
Comme à de vierges découvertes
Dans un jeu qui n'en finit pas
Pierres fanées murs sans écho
Je vous évite d'un sourire

Decour a été mis à mort.

10                    *A celle dont ils rêvent*

Neuf cent mille prisonniers
Cinq cent mille politiques
Un million de travailleurs

Maîtresse de leur sommeil
Donne-leur des forces d'homme
Le bonheur d'être sur terre
Donne-leur dans l'ombre immense
Les lèvres d'un amour doux
Comme l'oubli des souffrances

Maîtresse de leur sommeil
Fille femme sœur et mère
Aux seins gonflés de baisers
Donne-leur notre pays
Tel qu'ils l'ont toujours chéri
Un pays fou de la vie

Un pays où le vin chante
Où les moissons ont bon cœur
Où les enfants sont malins
Où les vieillards sont plus fins
Qu'arbres à fruits blancs de fleurs
Où l'on peut parler aux femmes

Neuf cent mille prisonniers
Cinq cent mille politiques
Un million de travailleurs

Maîtresse de leur sommeil
Neige noire de nuits blanches
A travers un feu exsangue
Sainte Aube à la canne blanche
Fais-leur voir un chemin neuf
Hors de leur prison de planches

Ils sont payés pour connaître
Les pires forces du mal
Pourtant ils ont tenu bon
Ils sont criblés de vertus
Tout autant que de blessures
Car il faut qu'ils se survivent

Maîtresse de leur repos
Maîtresse de leur éveil
Donne-leur la liberté
Mais garde-nous notre honte
D'avoir pu croire à la honte
Même pour l'anéantir.


11                        *Courage*

Paris a froid Paris a faim
Paris ne mange plus de marrons dans la rue
Paris a mis de vieux vêtements de vieille
Paris dort tout debout sans air dans le métro
Plus de malheur encore est imposé aux pauvres
Et la sagesse et la folie
De Paris malheureux
C'est l'air pur c'est le feu
C'est la beauté c'est la bonté
De ses travailleurs affamés
Ne crie pas au secours Paris
Tu es vivant d'une vie sans égale
Et derrière la nudité
De ta pâleur de ta maigreur
Tout ce qui est humain se révèle en tes yeux
Paris ma belle ville
Fine comme une aiguille forte comme une épée
Ingénue et savante
Tu ne supportes pas l'injustice
Pour toi c'est le seul désordre

Tu vas te libérer Paris
Paris tremblant comme une étoile
Notre espoir survivant
Tu vas te libérer de la fatigue et de la boue
Frères ayons du courage
Nous qui ne sommes pas casqués
Ni bottés ni gantés ni bien élevés
Un rayon s'allume en nos veines
Notre lumière nous revient
Les meilleurs d'entre nous sont morts pour nous
Et voici que leur sang retrouve notre cœur
Et c'est de nouveau le matin un matin de Paris
La pointe de la délivrance
L'espace du printemps naissant
La force idiote a le dessous
Ces esclaves nos ennemis
S'ils ont compris
S'ils sont capables de comprendre
Vont se lever.


12                    *Bêtes et méchants*

Venant du dedans
Venant du dehors
C'est nos ennemis
Ils viennent d'en haut
Ils viennent d'en bas
De près et de loin
De droite et de gauche
Habillés de vert
Habillés de gris
La veste trop courte
Le manteau trop long
La croix de travers
Grands de leurs fusils
Courts de leurs couteaux

Fiers de leurs espions
Forts de leurs bourreaux
Et gros de chagrin
Armés jusqu'à terre
Armés jusqu'en terre
Raides de saluts
Et raides de peur
Devant leurs bergers
Imbibés de bière
Imbibés de lune
Chantant gravement
La chanson des bottes
Ils ont oublié
La joie d'être aimé
Quand ils disent oui
Tout leur répond non
Quand ils parlent d'or
Tout se fait de plomb
Mais contre leur ombre
Tout se fera d'or
Tout rajeunira
Qu'ils partent qu'ils meurent
Leur mort nous suffit.

*

Nous aimons les hommes
Ils s'évaderont
Nous en prendrons soin
Au matin de gloire
D'un monde nouveau
D'un monde à l'endroit.


13                     *Chant Nazi*

Le vol fou d'un papillon
La fenêtre l'évasion

Le soleil interminable
La promesse inépuisable
Et qui se joue bien des balles
Cerne les yeux d'un frisson

L'arbre est neuf l'arbre est saignant
Mes enfants c'est le printemps
La dernière des saisons
Hâtez-vous profitez-en
C'est le bagne ou la prison
La fusillade ou le front

Dernière fête des mères
Le cœur cède saluons
Partout la mort la misère
Et l'Allemagne asservie
Et l'Allemagne accroupie
Dans le sang et la sanie
Dans les plaies qu'elle a creusées
Notre tâche est terminée

Ainsi chantent chantent bien
Les bons maîtres assassins.


14                    *Tuer*

Il tombe cette nuit
Une étrange paix sur Paris
Une paix d'yeux aveugles
De rêves sans couleur
Qui se cognent aux murs
Une paix de bras inutiles
De fronts vaincus
D'hommes absents
De femmes déjà passées
Pâles froides et sans larmes

Il tombe cette nuit
Dans le silence
Une étrange lueur sur Paris
Sur le bon vieux cœur de Paris
La lueur sourde du crime
Prémédité sauvage et pur
Du crime contre les bourreaux
Contre la mort.


15                     *Gabriel Péri*

Un homme est mort qui n'avait pour défense
Que ses bras ouverts à la vie
Un homme est mort qui n'avait d'autre route
Que celle où l'on hait les fusils
Un homme est mort qui continue la lutte
Contre la mort contre l'oubli

Car tout ce qu'il voulait
Nous le voulions aussi
Nous le voulons aujourd'hui
Que le bonheur soit la lumière
Au fond des yeux au fond du cœur
Et la justice sur la terre

Il y a des mots qui font vivre
Et ce sont des mots innocents
Le mot chaleur le mot confiance
Amour justice et le mot liberté
Le mot enfant et le mot gentillesse
Et certains noms de fleurs et certains noms de fruits
Le mot courage et le mot découvrir
Et le mot frère et le mot camarade
Et certains noms de pays de villages
Et certains noms de femmes et d'amis
Ajoutons-y Péri

Péri est mort pour ce qui nous fait vivre
Tutoyons-le sa poitrine est trouée
Mais grâce à lui nous nous connaissons mieux
Tutoyons-nous son espoir est vivant.


16                *A l'échelle humaine*

*à la mémoire du colonel*
*Fabien et à Laurent Casanova*
*qui m'a si bien parlé de lui*

On a tué un homme
Un homme un ancien enfant
Dans un grand paysage
Une tache de sang
Comme un soleil couchant
Un homme couronné
De femmes et d'enfants
Tout un idéal d'homme
Pour notre éternité

Il est tombé
Et son cœur s'est vidé
Ses yeux se sont vidés
Sa tête s'est vidée
Ses mains se sont ouvertes
Sans une plainte
Car il croyait au bonheur
Des autres
Car il avait répété
Je t'aime sur tous les tons
A sa mère à sa gardienne
A sa complice à son alliée
A la vie
Et il allait au combat
Contre les bourreaux des siens
Contre l'idée d'ennemi

Et même les pires jours
Il avait chéri sa peine
Sa nature était d'aimer
Et de respecter la vie
Sa nature était la mienne

Rien qu'un seul jet de courage
Rien que la grandeur du peuple
Et je t'aime finit mal
Mais il affirme la vie
Je t'aime c'était l'Espagne
Qui luttait pour le soleil
C'est la région parisienne
Avec ses chemins puérils
Avec ses enfants gentils
Et le premier attentat
Contre les soldats du mal
Contre la mort répugnante
C'est la première lumière
Dans la nuit des malheureux
Lumière toujours première
Toujours parfaite
Lumière de relation
Ronde de plus en plus souple
Étendue et animée
Graine et fleur et fruit et graine
Et je t'aime finit bien
Pour les hommes de demain.

17          *Les Vendeurs d'indulgence*

Ceux qui ont oublié le mal au nom du bien
Ceux qui n'ont pas de cœur nous prêchent le pardon
Les criminels leur sont indispensables
Ils croient qu'il faut de tout pour faire un monde.

*

Écoutez-les ils prêchent haut
Nul n'ose plus les faire taire
Ils ont des droits écoutez-les
Écoutez cet écho d'hier

*Qu'il résiste ou qu'il capitule*
*Un général en vaut un autre*
*Des Français habillés de vert*
*Sont quand même de fiers soldats*
*De bons canons pour l'ennemi*
*Sont quand même de bons canons*
*Et plus il possède d'esclaves*
*Plus le maître a de raisons d'être.*

\*

Les femmes d'Auschwitz les petits enfants juifs
Les terroristes à l'œil juste les otages
Ne pouvaient pas savoir par quel hideux miracle
La clémence serait ardemment invoquée.

\*

Il n'y a pas de pierre plus précieuse
Que le désir de venger l'innocent

Il n'y a pas de ciel plus éclatant
Que le matin où les traîtres succombent

Il n'y a pas de salut sur la terre
Tant que l'on peut pardonner aux bourreaux.

18                      *Faire vivre*

Ils étaient quelques-uns qui vivaient dans la nuit
En rêvant du ciel caressant

Ils étaient quelques-uns qui aimaient la forêt
Et qui croyaient au bois brûlant
L'odeur des fleurs les ravissait même de loin
La nudité de leurs désirs les recouvrait

Ils joignaient dans leur cœur le souffle mesuré
A ce rien d'ambition de la vie naturelle
Qui grandit dans l'été comme un été plus fort

Ils joignaient dans leur cœur l'espoir du temps qui vient
Et qui salue même de loin un autre temps
A des amours plus obstinées que le désert

Un tout petit peu de sommeil
Les rendait au soleil futur
Ils duraient ils savaient que vivre perpétue

Et leurs besoins obscurs engendraient la clarté.

*

Ils n'étaient que quelques-uns
Ils furent foule soudain

Ceci est de tous les temps.

# 2 AMATORY

19                    *L'Amoureuse*

Elle est debout sur mes paupières
Et ses cheveux sont dans les miens,
Elle a la forme de mes mains,
Elle a la couleur de mes yeux,
Elle s'engloutit dans mon ombre
Comme une pierre sur le ciel.

Elle a toujours les yeux ouverts
Et ne me laisse pas dormir.
Ses rêves en pleine lumière
Font s'évaporer les soleils,
Me font rire, pleurer et rire,
Parler sans avoir rien à dire.


20   Ta chevelure d'oranges dans le vide du monde
Dans le vide des vitres lourdes de silence
Et d'ombre où mes mains nues cherchent tous tes reflets.

La forme de ton cœur est chimérique
Et ton amour ressemble à mon désir perdu.
Ô soupirs d'ambre, rêves, regards.

Mais tu n'as pas toujours été avec moi. Ma mémoire
Est encore obscurcie de t'avoir vue venir
Et partir. Le temps se sert de mots comme l'amour.

21   La courbe de tes yeux fait le tour de mon cœur,
     Un rond de danse et de douceur,
     Auréole du temps, berceau nocturne et sûr,
     Et si je ne sais plus tout ce que j'ai vécu
     C'est que tes yeux ne m'ont pas toujours vu.

     Feuilles de jour et mousse de rosée,
     Roseaux du vent, sourires parfumés,
     Ailes couvrant le monde de lumière,
     Bateaux chargés du ciel et de la mer,
     Chasseurs des bruits et sources des couleurs,

     Parfums éclos d'une couvée d'aurores
     Qui gît toujours sur la paille des astres,
     Comme le jour dépend de l'innocence
     Le monde entier dépend de tes yeux purs
     Et tout mon sang coule dans leurs regards.


22             *Celle de toujours, toute*

     Si je vous dis: «j'ai tout abandonné»
     C'est qu'elle n'est pas celle de mon corps,
     Je ne m'en suis jamais vanté,
     Ce n'est pas vrai
     Et la brume de fond où je me meus
     Ne sait jamais si j'ai passé.

     L'éventail de sa bouche, le reflet de ses yeux,
     Je suis le seul à en parler,
     Je suis le seul qui soit cerné
     Par ce miroir si nul où l'air circule à travers moi
     Et l'air a un visage, un visage aimé,
     Un visage aimant, ton visage,

A toi qui n'as pas de nom et que les autres ignorent,
La mer te dit: sur moi, le ciel te dit: sur moi,
Les astres te devinent, les nuages t'imaginent
Et le sang répandu aux meilleurs moments,
Le sang de la générosité
Te porte avec délices.

Je chante la grande joie de te chanter,
La grande joie de t'avoir ou de ne pas t'avoir,
La candeur de t'attendre, l'innocence de te connaître,
Ô toi qui supprimes l'oubli, l'espoir et l'ignorance,
Qui supprimes l'absence et qui me mets au monde,
Je chante pour chanter, je t'aime pour chanter
Le mystère où l'amour me crée et se délivre.

Tu es pure, tu es encore plus pure que moi-même.


23    Je te l'ai dit pour les nuages
Je te l'ai dit pour l'arbre de la mer
Pour chaque vague pour les oiseaux dans les feuilles
Pour les cailloux du bruit
Pour les mains familières
Pour l'œil qui devient visage ou paysage
Et le sommeil lui rend le ciel de sa couleur
Pour toute la nuit bue
Pour la grille des routes
Pour la fenêtre ouverte pour un front découvert
Je te l'ai dit pour tes pensées pour tes paroles
Toute caresse toute confiance se survivent.


24    Le front aux vitres comme font les veilleurs de chagrin
Ciel dont j'ai dépassé la nuit

Plaines toutes petites dans mes mains ouvertes
Dans leur double horizon inerte indifférent
Le front aux vitres comme font les veilleurs de chagrin
Je te cherche par-delà l'attente
Par-delà moi-même
Et je ne sais plus tant je t'aime
Lequel de nous deux est absent.

25        Voyage du silence
          De mes mains à tes yeux

          Et dans tes cheveux
          Où des filles d'osier
          S'adossent au soleil
          Remuent les lèvres
          Et laissent l'ombre à quatre feuilles
          Gagner leur cœur chaud de sommeil.

26            *Par une nuit nouvelle*

          Femme avec laquelle j'ai vécu
          Femme avec laquelle je vis
          Femme avec laquelle je vivrai
          Toujours la même
          Il te faut un manteau rouge
          Des gants rouges un masque rouge
          Et des bas noirs
          Des raisons des preuves
          De te voir toute nue
          Nudité pure ô parure parée

          Seins ô mon cœur

27                    *Au revoir*

Devant moi cette main qui défait les orages
Qui défrise et qui fait fleurir les plantes grimpantes
Avec sûreté est-ce la tienne est-ce un signal
Quand le silence pèse encore sur les mares au fond des
   puits tout au fond du matin.

Jamais décontenancée jamais surprise est-ce ta main
Qui jure sur chaque feuille la paume au soleil
Le prenant à témoin est-ce ta main qui jure
De recevoir la moindre ondée et d'en accepter le déluge
Sans l'ombre d'un éclair passé
Est-ce ta main ce souvenir foudroyant au soleil.

Prends garde la place du trésor est perdue
Les oiseaux de nuit sans mouvement dans leur parure
Ne fixent rien que l'insomnie aux nerfs assassins
Dénouée est-ce ta main qui est ainsi indifférente
Au crépuscule qui laisse tout échapper.

Toutes les rivières trouvent des charmes à leur enfance
Toutes les rivières reviennent du bain
Les voitures affolées parent de leurs roues le sein des
   places
Est-ce ta main qui fait la roue
Sur les places qui ne tournent plus
Ta main dédaigneuse de l'eau des caresses
Ta main dédaigneuse de ma confiance de mon insouciance
Ta main qui ne saura jamais me détourner de toi.


28                    *Une pour toutes*

Une ou plusieurs
L'azur couché sur l'orage
La neige sur les oiseaux
Les bruits de la peur dans les bois revêches

Une ou plusieurs
Dans les coques de glaise on a semé des corbeaux
Aux ailes fanées au bec de tremblement de terre
Ils ont cueilli les fantastiques roses rousses de l'orage

Une ou plusieurs
La collerette du soleil
L'immense fraise du soleil
Sur le goulot d'une clairière

Une ou plusieurs
Plus sensibles à leur enfance
Qu'à la pluie et au beau temps
Plus douces à connaître
Que le sommeil en pente douce
Loin de l'ennui

Une ou plusieurs
Dans des miroirs câlins
Où leur voix le matin se déchire comme un linge

Une ou plusieurs
Faites de pierre qui s'effrite
Et de plume qui s'éparpille
Faites de ronces faites de lin d'alcool d'écume
De rires de sanglots de négligences de tourments ridicules
Faites de chair et d'yeux véritables sans doute

Une ou plusieurs
Avec tous leurs défauts tous leurs mérites
Des femmes

Une ou plusieurs
Le visage ganté de lierre
Tentantes comme du pain frais
Toutes les femmes qui m'émeuvent
Parées de ce que j'ai souhaité

Parées de calme et de fraîcheur
Parées de sel d'eau de soleil
De tendresse d'audace et de mille caprices
De mille chaînes

Une ou plusieurs
Dans tous mes rêves
Une nouvelle fleur des bois
Fleur barbare aux pistils en fagot
Qui s'ouvre dans le cercle ardent de ses délires
Dans la nuit meurtrie

Une ou plusieurs

Une jeunesse à en mourir
Une jeunesse violente inquiète et saturée d'ennui
Qu'elle a partagé avec moi
Sans se soucier des autres.


29                    *Telle femme,*
          *principe de vie, interlocutrice idéale*

Veux-tu voir
La forme obscure du soleil
Les contours de la vie
Ou bien te laisser éblouir
Par le feu qui mêle tout
Le flambeau passeur de pudeurs
En chair en or ce beau geste

L'erreur est aussi inconnue
Que les limites du printemps
La tentation est prodigieuse
Tout se touche tout te traverse
Ce ne fut d'abord qu'un tonnerre d'encens
Ce que tu aimes le plus

La louange belle à quatre
Belle nue immobile
Violon muet mais palpable
Je te parle de voir

Je te parlerai de tes yeux
Sois sans visage si tu veux
De leur couleur contre le gré
Des pierres lumineuses
Décolorées
Devant l'homme que tu conquiers
Son enthousiasme aveugle
Règne naïvement comme une source
Dans le désert

Entre les plages de la nuit et les vagues du jour
Entre la terre et l'eau
Nulle ride à combler
Nul chemin possible

Entre tes yeux et les images que j'y vois
Il y a tout ce que j'en pense
Moi-même indéracinable
Comme une plante qui s'amasse
Qui simule un rocher parmi d'autres rochers
Ce que je porte de certain
Toi tout entière
Tout ce que tu regardes
Tout

Ceci est un bateau
Qui va sur une rivière douce
Il porte des femmes qui jouent
Et des graines qui patientent
Ceci est un cheval qui descend la colline
Ou bien une flamme qui s'élève
Un grand rire pieds nus dans une cour misérable

Un comble de l'automne des verdures amadouées
Un oiseau acharné à mettre des ailes à son nid
Un matin qui disperse des lampes de rosée
Pour éveiller les champs
Ceci est une ombrelle
Et ceci la toilette
D'une dentellière plus séduisante qu'un bouquet
Au son des cloches de l'arc-en-ciel

Ceci déjoue l'immensité
Ceci n'a jamais assez de place
La bienvenue est toujours ailleurs
Avec la foudre avec le flot
Qui s'accompagnent
De méduses et d'incendies
Complaisants à merveille
Ils détruisent l'échafaudage
Surmonté d'un triste drapeau de couleur
Une étoile limite
Dont les doigts sont paralysés

Je parle de te voir
Je te sais vivante
Tout existe tout est visible
Il n'y a pas une goutte de nuit dans tes yeux

Je vis dans une lumière exclusive la tienne.


30                        *Le Baiser*

Un coq à la porte de l'aube
Un coq battant de cloche
Brise le temps nocturne sur des galets de promptitude

Un lancer de ramages
Entre deux transparences inégales

On ne va pas si tôt lever la tête
Vers la lumière qui s'assemble
Mais la baisser
Sur une bouche plus vorace qu'une murène
Sur une bouche qui se cache sous les paupières
Et qui bientôt se cachera derrière les yeux
Porteuse de rêves nouveaux
La plus douce des charrues
Inutile indispensable
Elle sait la place de chaque chose
Dans le silence
Collier rompu des mots rebelles
Une autre bouche pour litière
Compagne des herbes fiévreuses
Ennemie des pièges
Sauvage et bonne formée pour tous
Et pour personne
Bouche oublieuse du langage
Bouche éclairée par les mirages de la nuit

Le premier pas sur cette route franche
Monotone comme un enfant
Mille orchidées à l'infini
Brillant brûlant pont vivant
Image écho reflet d'une naissance perpétuelle

C'est gagner un instant
Pour ne plus jamais douter de durer.

31          Tu te lèves l'eau se déplie
            Tu te couches l'eau s'épanouit

Tu es l'eau détournée de ses abîmes
Tu es la terre qui prend racine
Et sur laquelle tout s'établit

Tu fais des bulles de silence dans le désert des bruits
Tu chantes des hymnes nocturnes sur les cordes de
    l'arc-en-ciel
Tu es partout tu abolis toutes les routes

Tu sacrifies le temps
A l'éternelle jeunesse de la flamme exacte
Qui voile la nature en la reproduisant

Femme tu mets au monde un corps toujours pareil
Le tien

Tu es la ressemblance.


32                    *Sans âge*

Nous approchons
Dans les forêts
Prenez la rue du matin
Montez les marches de la brume

Nous approchons
La terre en a le cœur crispé

Encore un jour à mettre au monde.

                            *

Le ciel s'élargira
Nous en avions assez
D'habiter dans les ruines du sommeil
Dans l'ombre basse du repos
De la fatigue de l'abandon

La terre reprendra la forme de nos corps vivants
Le vent nous subira
Le soleil et la nuit passeront dans nos yeux
Sans jamais les changer

Notre espace certain notre air pur est de taille
A combler le retard creusé par l'habitude
Nous aborderons tous une mémoire nouvelle
Nous parlerons ensemble un langage sensible.

                         *


Ô mes frères contraires gardant dans vos prunelles
La nuit infuse et son horreur
Où vous ai-je laissés
Avec vos lourdes mains dans l'huile paresseuse
De vos actes anciens
Avec si peu d'espoir que la mort a raison
Ô mes frères perdus
Moi je vais vers la vie j'ai l'apparence d'homme
Pour prouver que le monde est fait à ma mesure

Et je ne suis pas seul
Mille images de moi multiplient ma lumière
Mille regards pareils égalisent la chair
C'est l'oiseau c'est l'enfant c'est le roc c'est la plaine
Qui se mêlent à nous
L'or éclate de rire de se voir hors du gouffre
L'eau le feu se dénudent pour une seule saison
Il n'y a plus d'éclipse au front de l'univers.

                         *


Mains par nos mains reconnues
Lèvres à nos lèvres confondues
Les premières chaleurs florales
Alliées à la fraîcheur du sang

Le prisme respire avec nous
Aube abondante
Au sommet de chaque herbe reine
Au sommet des mousses à la pointe des neiges
Des vagues des sables bouleversés
Des enfances persistantes
Hors de toutes les cavernes
Hors de nous-mêmes.


33                    *Je ne suis pas seul*

Chargée
De fruits légers aux lèvres
Parée
De mille fleurs variées
Glorieuse
Dans les bras du soleil
Heureuse
D'un oiseau familier
Ravie
D'une goutte de pluie
Plus belle
Que le ciel du matin
Fidèle

Je parle d'un jardin
Je rêve

Mais j'aime justement.


34                    *Nous n'importe où*

L'oiseau s'arrête guette une proie invisible
Il chasse il donne à ses petits
De quoi chanter voler dormir

Au dur contact de la forêt fermée
Il préfère les champs humides
Chargés des derniers brins du jour

La fine trame de la vie
Couvre doucement ton visage
Et tu tiens dans cette corbeille
Nos moyens nos raisons de vivre
Tu es aussi sage que belle
A toi vont les mots les plus beaux

Nous parlerons ce soir de nous et des oiseaux
Nous n'écouterons pas la longue et sourde histoire
Des hommes chassés de chez eux
Par la mort aux mâchoires d'or
Des hommes moins fiers que des bêtes
Qui suivent le malheur partout
Que n'arrivent-ils donc tout nus
Dans un asile de clarté comme le nôtre

Nous prenons souci l'un de l'autre
Jour après jour nous gardons notre vie
Comme un oiseau sa forme éclose
Et son plaisir
Parmi tant d'oiseaux à venir.


35          *«Je veux qu'elle soit reine!»*

*à Nusch*

Un village une ville et l'écho de ma voix

L'oreille fascinée efface le silence
Écoute sur le toit les voleurs de beau temps
Gorgés de vent de pluie
Ils venaient de la mer ils allaient vers le ciel

Ils sont restés en route
Écoute pour apprendre à dire les raisons
De ce que tu entends

Dans la rue
D'un homme on en fait deux
Et de toutes les femmes on dégage l'unique
A qui je parle
A toi écoute je réponds
A toutes tes paroles aux premières aux dernières
Aux murmures aux cris à la source au sommet
Je te réponds mon amour sans limites

Un village une ville et l'écho de ta voix
Taillant les villages les villes les partageant
La grande règle
Ce qui est digne d'être aimé
Contre ce qui s'anéantit

Sans songer à d'autres soleils
Que celui qui brille en mes bras
Sans t'appeler d'un autre nom
Que notre amour
Je vis et règne entre des murs
Je vis et règne hors des murs
Sur les bois sur la mer sur les champs sur les monts
Et sur les yeux et sur les voix qui les répètent

Habitante d'un monde où sans toi je n'ai rien
Ton cœur qui déjà dort oublie tout sauf mon cœur
Dehors nos souvenirs nuits à flanc de journées
Agitent nos liens sans pouvoir les briser.


36                          *L'Extase*

Je suis devant ce paysage féminin
Comme un enfant devant le feu

Souriant vaguement et les larmes aux yeux
Devant ce paysage où tout remue en moi
Où des miroirs s'embuent où des miroirs s'éclairent
Reflétant deux corps nus saison contre saison

J'ai tant de raisons de me perdre
Sur cette terre sans chemins et sous ce ciel sans horizon
Belles raisons que j'ignorais hier
Et que je n'oublierai jamais
Belles clés des regards clés filles d'elles-mêmes
Devant ce paysage où la nature est mienne

Devant le feu le premier feu
Bonne raison maîtresse
Étoile identifiée
Et sur la terre et sous le ciel hors de mon cœur et dans mon
   cœur
Second bourgeon première feuille verte
Que la mer couvre de ses ailes
Et le soleil au bout de tout venant de nous

Je suis devant ce paysage féminin
Comme une branche dans le feu.


37                    *Les Limites du malheur*

            Mes yeux soudain horriblement
            Ne voient pas plus loin que moi
            Je fais des gestes dans le vide
            Je suis comme un aveugle-né
            De son unique nuit témoin

            La vie soudain horriblement
            N'est plus à la mesure du temps
            Mon désert contredit l'espace

Désert pourri désert livide
De ma morte que j'envie

J'ai dans mon corps vivant les ruines de l'amour
Ma morte dans sa robe au col taché de sang.


38                    *Ma morte vivante*


Dans mon chagrin rien n'est en mouvement
J'attends personne ne viendra
Ni de jour ni de nuit
Ni jamais plus de ce qui fut moi-même

Mes yeux se sont séparés de tes yeux
Ils perdent leur confiance ils perdent leur lumière
Ma bouche s'est séparée de ta bouche
Ma bouche s'est séparée du plaisir
Et du sens de l'amour et du sens de la vie
Mes mains se sont séparées de tes mains
Mes mains laissent tout échapper
Mes pieds se sont séparés de tes pieds
Ils n'avanceront plus il n'y a plus de routes
Ils ne connaîtront plus mon poids ni le repos

Il m'est donné de voir ma vie finir
Avec la tienne
Ma vie en ton pouvoir
Que j'ai crue infinie

Et l'avenir mon seul espoir c'est mon tombeau
Pareil au tien cerné d'un monde indifférent

J'étais si près de toi que j'ai froid près des autres.

39        *Négation de la poésie*

J'ai pris de toi tout le souci tout le tourment
Que l'on peut prendre à travers tout à travers rien
Aurais-je pu ne pas t'aimer
Ô toi rien que la gentillesse
Comme une pêche après une autre pêche
Aussi fondantes que l'été


Tout le souci tout le tourment
De vivre encore et d'être absent
D'écrire ce poème
Au lieu du poème vivant
Que je n'écrirai pas
Puisque tu n'es pas là


Les plus ténus dessins du feu
Préparent l'incendie ultime
Les moindres miettes de pain
Suffisent aux mourants


J'ai connu la vertu vivante
J'ai connu le bien incarné
Je refuse ta mort mais j'accepte la mienne
Ton ombre qui s'étend sur moi
Je voudrais en faire un jardin


L'arc débandé nous sommes de la même nuit
Et je veux continuer ton immobilité
Et le discours inexistant
Qui commence avec toi qui finira en moi
Avec moi volontaire obstiné révolté
Amoureux comme toi des charmes de la terre.

40                         *Notre vie* [I]

Notre vie tu l'as faite elle est ensevelie
Aurore d'une ville un beau matin de mai
Sur laquelle la terre a refermé son poing
Aurore en moi dix-sept années toujours plus claires
Et la mort entre en moi comme dans un moulin

Notre vie disais-tu si contente de vivre
Et de donner la vie à ce que nous aimions
Mais la mort a rompu l'équilibre du temps
La mort qui vient la mort qui va la mort vécue
La mort visible boit et mange à mes dépens

Morte visible Nusch invisible et plus dure
Que la soif et la faim à mon corps épuisé
Masque de neige sur la terre et sous la terre
Source des larmes dans la nuit masque d'aveugle
Mon passé se dissout je fais place au silence.


41                    *Vivante et morte séparée*

Vivante et morte séparée j'ai trébuché
Sur une tombe sur un corps
Qui soulève à peine la terre
Sur un corps dont j'étais construit
Sur la bouche qui me parlait
Et sur les yeux pourris de toutes les vertus
Mes mains mes pieds étaient les siens
Et mes désirs et mon poème étaient les siens
J'ai trébuché sur sa gaîté sur sa bonté
Qui maintenant ont les rigueurs de son squelette
Mon amour est de plus en plus concret il est en terre
Et non ailleurs j'imagine son odeur
Mon amour mon petit ma couronne d'odeurs
Tu n'avais rien de rien à faire avec la mort

Ton crâne n'avait pas connu la nuit des temps
Mon éphémère écoute je suis là je t'accompagne
Je te parle notre langue elle est minime et va d'un coup
Du grand soleil au grand soleil et nous mourons d'être
    vivants
Ecoute ici c'est notre chien ici notre maison
Ici c'est notre lit ici ceux qui nous aiment
Tous les produits de notre cœur de notre sang
Et de nos sens et de nos rêves
Je n'oublie rien de ces oiseaux de grande espèce
Qui nous guident qui nous enlèvent
Et qui font des trous dans l'azur
Comme volcans en pleine terre
Ma fille mon garçon petite mère et petit père
Mon poème ce soir aurait pu te distraire
Avec les mots précis que tu es fière de comprendre
Avec les arrêts brusques des péripéties
Et les zibelines vives de la coquetterie
Et l'abasourdissante écume de la mer
Et la réminiscence et l'oubli délétère
Mon corps vivant charmant ma raison ma déraison
Ma séduction ma solitude mon plaisir et ma souffrance
Ma modestie et mon orgueil ma perversion et mon mérite
Toute petite et délabrée parfaite et pure
Pareille à un verre d'eau qui sera toujours bu
Je ne dors pas je suis tombé j'ai trébuché sur ton absence
Je suis sans feu sans force près de toi
Je suis le dessous de la bête je m'accroche
A notre chute à notre ruine
Je suis au-dessous de tes restes
J'aspire à ton néant je voudrais voir mon front
Comme un caillou loin dans la terre
Comme un bateau fondu dans l'eau
Mon petit qui pourtant m'engendras en orage
Me convertis en homme et m'aimas comme un sage
Ma voix n'a pas d'écho j'ai honte de parler
Je souffre pour toujours de ton silence ô mon amour.

42          *Dominique aujourd'hui présente*

Toutes les choses au hasard
Tous les mots dits sans y penser
Et qui sont pris comme ils sont dits
Et nul n'y perd et nul n'y gagne

Les sentiments à la dérive
Et l'effort le plus quotidien
Le vague souvenir des songes
L'avenir en butte à demain

Les mots coincés dans un enfer
De roues usées de lignes mortes
Les choses grises et semblables
Les hommes tournant dans le vent

Muscles voyants squelette intime
Et la vapeur des sentiments
Le cœur réglé comme un cercueil
Les espoirs réduits à néant

*

Tu es venue l'après-midi crevait la terre
Et la terre et les hommes ont changé de sens
Et je me suis trouvé réglé comme un aimant
Réglé comme une vigne

A l'infini notre chemin le but des autres
Des abeilles volaient futures de leur miel
Et j'ai multiplié mes désirs de lumière
Pour en comprendre la raison

Tu es venue j'étais très triste j'ai dit oui
C'est à partir de toi que j'ai dit oui au monde
Petite fille je t'aimais comme un garçon
Ne peut aimer que son enfance

Avec la force d'un passé très loin très pur
Avec le feu d'une chanson sans fausse note
La pierre intacte et le courant furtif du sang
Dans la gorge et les lèvres

Tu es venue la vœu de vivre avait un corps
Il creusait la nuit lourde il caressait les ombres
Pour dissoudre leur boue et fondre leurs glaçons
Comme un œil qui voit clair

L'herbe fine figeait le vol des hirondelles
Et l'automne pesait dans le sac des ténèbres
Tu es venue les rives libéraient le fleuve
Pour le mener jusqu'à la mer

Tu es venue plus haute au fond de ma douleur
Que l'arbre séparé de la forêt sans air
Et le cri du chagrin du doute s'est brisé
Devant le jour de notre amour

Gloire l'ombre et la honte ont cédé au soleil
Le poids s'est allégé le fardeau s'est fait rire
Gloire le souterrain est devenu sommet
La misère s'est effacée

La place d'habitude où je m'abêtissais
Le couloir sans réveil l'impasse et la fatigue
Se sont mis à briller d'un feu battant des mains
L'éternité s'est dépliée

Ô toi mon agitée et ma calme pensée
Mon silence sonore et mon écho secret
Mon aveugle voyante et ma vue dépassée
Je n'ai plus eu que ta présence

Tu m'as couvert de ta confiance.

43    *Je t'aime*

Je t'aime pour toutes les femmes que je n'ai pas connues
Je t'aime pour tous les temps où je n'ai pas vécu
Pour l'odeur du grand large et l'odeur du pain chaud
Pour la neige qui fond pour les premières fleurs
Pour les animaux purs que l'homme n'effraie pas
Je t'aime pour aimer
Je t'aime pour toutes les femmes que je n'aime pas

Qui me reflète sinon toi moi-même je me vois si peu
Sans toi je ne vois rien qu'une étendue déserte
Entre autrefois et aujourd'hui
Il y a eu toutes ces morts que j'ai franchies sur de la paille
Je n'ai pas pu percer le mur de mon miroir
Il m'a fallu apprendre mot par mot la vie
Comme on oublie

Je t'aime pour ta sagesse qui n'est pas la mienne
Pour la santé
Je t'aime contre tout ce qui n'est qu'illusion
Pour ce cœur immortel que je ne détiens pas
Tu crois être le doute et tu n'es que raison
Tu es le grand soleil qui me monte à la tête
Quand je suis sûr de moi.

# 3  PICTORIAL

44                          *Giorgio de Chirico*

Un mur dénonce un autre mur
Et l'ombre me défend de mon ombre peureuse.
Ô tour de mon amour autour de mon amour,
Tous les murs filaient blanc autour de mon silence.

Toi, que défendais-tu? Ciel insensible et pur
Tremblant tu m'abritais. La lumière en relief
Sur le ciel qui n'est plus le miroir du soleil,
Les étoiles de jour parmi les feuilles vertes,

Le souvenir de ceux qui parlaient sans savoir,
Maîtres de ma faiblesse et je suis à leur place
Avec des yeux d'amour et des mains trop fidèles
Pour dépeupler un monde dont je suis absent.


45                          *Pablo Picasso*

Les armes du sommeil ont creusé dans la nuit
Les sillons merveilleux qui séparent nos têtes.
A travers le diamant, toute médaille est fausse,
Sous le ciel éclatant, la terre est invisible.

Le visage du cœur a perdu ses couleurs
Et le soleil nous cherche et la neige est aveugle.
Si nous l'abandonnons, l'horizon a des ailes
Et nos regards au loin dissipent les erreurs.

46                    *André Masson*

La cruauté se noue et la douceur agile se dénoue.
L'aimant des ailes prend des visages bien clos, les
flammes de la terre s'évadent par les seins et le jasmin
des mains s'ouvre sur une étoile.

Le ciel tout engourdi, le ciel qui se dénoue n'est plus
sur nous. L'oubli, mieux que le soir, l'efface. Privée de
sang et de reflets, la cadence des tempes et des colonnes
subsiste.

Les lignes de la main, autant de branches dans le
vent tourbillonnant. Rampe des mois d'hiver, jour pâle
d'insomnie, mais aussi, dans les chambres les plus
secrètes de l'ombre, la guirlande d'un corps autour de
sa splendeur.

47                    *Paul Klee*

Sur la pente fatale, le voyageur profite
De la faveur du jour, verglas et sans cailloux,
Et les yeux bleus d'amour, découvre sa saison
Qui porte à tous les doigts de grands astres en bague.

Sur la plage la mer a laissé ses oreilles
Et le sable creusé la place d'un beau crime.
Le supplice est plus dur aux bourreaux qu'aux victimes
Les couteaux sont des signes et les balles des larmes.

48                    *Max Ernst* [2]

Dévoré par les plumes et soumis à la mer
Il a laissé passer son ombre dans le vol
Des oiseaux de la liberté.

Il a laissé
La rampe à ceux qui tombent sous la pluie,
Il a laissé leur toit à tous ceux qui se vérifient.

Son corps était en ordre,
Le corps des autres est venu disperser
Cette ordonnance qu'il tenait
De la première empreinte de son sang sur terre.

Ses yeux sont dans un mur
Et son visage est leur lourde parure.
Un mensonge de plus du jour,
Une nuit de plus, il n'y a plus d'aveugles.


49                    *Georges Braque*

Un oiseau s'envole,
Il rejette les nues comme un voile inutile.
Il n'a jamais craint la lumière,
Enfermé dans son vol,
Il n'a jamais eu d'ombre.


Coquilles des moissons brisées par le soleil.
Toutes les feuilles dans les bois disent oui,
Elles ne savent dire que oui,
Toute question, toute réponse
Et la rosée coule au fond de ce oui.


Un homme aux yeux légers décrit le ciel d'amour.
Il en rassemble les merveilles
Comme des feuilles dans un bois,
Comme des oiseaux dans leur ailes
Et des hommes dans le sommeil.

50                        *Joan Miró*

Soleil de proie prisonnier de ma tête,
Enlève la colline, enlève la forêt.
Le ciel est plus beau que jamais.

Les libellules des raisins
Lui donnent des formes précises
Que je dissipe d'un geste.

Nuages du premier jour,
Nuages insensibles et que rien n'autorise,
Leurs graines brûlent
Dans les feux de paille de mes regards.

A la fin, pour se couvrir d'une aube
Il faudra que le ciel soit aussi pur que la nuit.

51                        *Yves Tanguy*

Un soir tous les soirs et ce soir comme les autres
Près de la nuit hermaphrodite
A croissance à peine retardée
Les lampes et leur venaison sont sacrifiées
Mais dans l'œil calciné des lynx et des hiboux
Le grand soleil interminable
Crève-cœur des saisons
Le corbeau familial
La puissance de voir que la terre environne.

Il y a des étoiles en relief sur eau froide
Plus noires que la nuit
Ainsi sur l'heure comme une fin l'aurore
Toutes illusions à fleur de mémoire
Toutes les feuilles à l'ombre des parfums.

Et les filles des mains ont beau pour m'endormir
Cambrer leur taille ouvrir les anémones de leurs seins
Je ne prends rien dans ces filets de chair et de frissons
Du bout du monde au crépuscule d'aujourd'hui
Rien ne résiste à mes images désolées.

En guise d'ailes le silence a des plaines gelées
Que le moindre désir fait craquer
La nuit qui se retourne les découvre
Et les rejette à l'horizon.

Nous avions décidé que rien ne se définirait
Que selon le doigt posé par hasard sur les commandes
    d'un appareil brisé.


52              *Salvador Dali*

C'est en tirant sur la corde des villes en fanant
Les provinces que le délié des sexes
Accroît les sentiments rugueux du père
En quête d'une végétation nouvelle
Dont les nuits boule de neige
Interdisent à l'adresse de montrer le bout mobile de son
    nez.

C'est en lissant les graines imperceptibles des désirs
Que l'aiguille s'arrête complaisamment
Sur la dernière minute de l'araignée et du pavot
Sur la céramique de l'iris et du point de suspension
Que l'aiguille se noue sur la fausse audace
De l'arrêt dans les gares et du doigt de la pudeur.

C'est en pavant les rues de nids d'oiseaux
Que le piano des mêlées de géants
Fait passer au profit de la famille
Les chants interminables des changements de grandeur
De deux êtres qui se quittent.

C'est en acceptant de se servir des outils de la rouille
En constatant nonchalamment la bonne foi du métal
Que les mains s'ouvrent aux délices des bouquets
Et autres petits diables des villégiatures
Au fond des poches rayées de rouge.


C'est en s'accrochant à un rideau de mouches
Que la pêcheuse malingre se défend des marins
Elle ne s'intéresse pas à la mer bête et ronde comme une
    pomme
Le bois qui manque la forêt qui n'est pas là
La rencontre qui n'a pas lieu et pour boire
La verdure dans les verres et la bouche qui n'est faite
Que pour pleurer une arme le seul terme de comparaison
Avec la table avec le verre avec les larmes
Et l'ombre forge le squelette du cristal de roche.


C'est pour ne pas laisser ces yeux les nôtres vides entre
    nous
Qu'elle tend ses bras nus
La fille sans bijoux la fille à la peau nue
Il faudrait bien par-ci par-là des rochers des vagues
Des femmes pour nous distraire pour nous habiller
Ou des cerises d'émeraudes dans le lait de la rosée.


Tant d'aubes brèves dans les mains
Tant de gestes maniaques pour dissiper l'insomnie
Sous la rebondissante nuit du linge
Face à l'escalier dont chaque marche est le plateau d'une
    balance
Face aux oiseaux dressés contre les torrents
L'étoile lourde du beau temps s'ouvre les veines.

53                    *Man Ray*

L'orage d'une robe qui s'abat
Puis un corps simple sans nuages
Ainsi venez me dire tous vos charmes
Vous qui avez eu votre part de bonheur
Et qui pleurez souvent le sort sinistre de celui qui vous a
    rendue si heureuse


Vous qui n'avez pas envie de raisonner
Vous qui n'avez pas su faire un homme
Sans en aimer un autre


Dans les espaces de marées d'un corps qui se dévêt
A la mamelle du crépuscule ressemblant
L'œil fait la chaîne sur les dunes négligées
Où les fontaines tiennent dans leur griffes des mains nues
Vestiges du front nu joues pâles sous les cils de l'horizon
Une larme fusée fiancée au passé
Savoir que la lumière fut fertile
Des hirondelles enfantines prennent la terre pour le ciel


La chambre noire où tous les cailloux du froid sont à vif
Ne dis pas que tu n'as pas peur
Ton regard est à la hauteur de mon épaule
Tu es trop belle pour prêcher la chasteté


Dans la chambre noire où le blé même
Naît de la gourmandise


Reste immobile
Et tu es seule.

54                    *René Magritte*

Marches de l'œil
A travers les barreaux des formes
Un escalier perpétuel
Le repos qui n'existe pas
Une des marches est cachée par un nuage
Une autre par un grand couteau
Une autre par un arbre qui se déroule
Comme un tapis
Sans gestes

Toutes les marches sont cachées

On a semé les feuilles vertes
Champs immenses forêts déduites
Au coucher des rampes de plomb
Au niveau des clairières
Dans le lait léger du matin

Le sable abreuve de rayons
Les silhouettes des miroirs
Leurs épaules pâles et froides
Leurs sourires décoratifs

L'arbre est teinté de fruits invulnérables.


55                    *A Marc Chagall*

Âne ou vache coq ou cheval
Jusqu'à la peau d'un violon
Homme chanteur un seul oiseau
Danseur agile avec sa femme

Couple trempé dans son printemps

L'or de l'herbe le plomb du ciel
Séparés par les flammes bleues
De la santé de la rosée
Le sang s'irise le cœur tinte

Un couple le premier reflet

Et dans un souterrain de neige
La vigne opulente dessine
Un visage aux lèvres de lune
Qui n'a jamais dormi la nuit.


56                        *A Fernand Léger*

De la première couleur nue
Au quart de tour de toute forme
A l'équilibre et l'œil se régénère
Foin du granit et des aiguilles vives
Le mouvement délire dans le vide

L'orage forge des vacances
Au ciel pur taché de silence
Un aigle y est lié à jamais
Et sur la terre la nature
Pèse de tout son poids de terre

Multipliés à l'infini
Les feuilles rôdent sur les arbres
Les hommes rôdent sur les routes
Les chaînes se nouent et s'affalent
La femme reproduit la femme

Reproduira l'homme au carré

Mais un immense drapeau bat
Comme un miroir dans la lumière
Célébrant à la fois défaites et victoires
Dans les mains de celui qui sans trembler regarde

La coupe de son cœur sur le tranchant du temps.

# 4   ANIMAL

*Animal rit*

Le monde rit,
Le monde est heureux, content et joyeux.
La bouche s'ouvre, ouvre ses ailes et retombe.
Les bouches jeunes retombent,
Les bouches vieilles retombent.

Un animal rit aussi,
Étendant la joie de ses contorsions.
Dans tous les endroits de la terre
Le poil remue, la laine danse
Et les oiseaux perdent leurs plumes.

Un animal rit aussi,
Et saute loin de lui-même.
Le monde rit,
Un animal rit aussi,
Un animal s'enfuit.


*Cheval*

Cheval seul, cheval perdu,
Malade de la pluie, vibrant d'insectes,
Cheval seul, vieux cheval.
Aux fêtes du galop,
Son élan serait vers la terre,
Il se tuerait.

Et, fidèle aux cailloux,
Cheval seul attend la nuit
Pour n'être pas obligé
De voir clair et de se sauver.

59         *Vache* [I]

On ne mène pas la vache
A la verdure rase et sèche,
A la verdure sans caresses.

L'herbe qui la reçoit
Doit être douce comme un fil de soie,
Un fil de soie doux comme un fil de lait.

Mère ignorée,
Pour les enfants, ce n'est pas le déjeuner,
Mais le lait sur l'herbe

L'herbe devant la vache,
L'enfant devant le lait.

60         *Porc*

Du soleil sur le dos, du soleil sur le ventre,
La tête grosse et immobile
Comme un canon,
Le porc travaille.

61         *Poule* [I]

Hélas! ma sœur, bête bête,
Ce n'est pas à cause de ton chant,
De ton chant pour l'œuf
Que l'homme te croit bonne.

62                          *Poisson*

Les poissons, les nageurs, les bateaux
Transforment l'eau.
L'eau est douce et ne bouge
Que pour ce qui la touche.

Le poisson avance
Comme un doigt dans un gant,
Le nageur danse lentement
Et la voile respire.

Mais l'eau douce bouge
Pour ce qui la touche,
Pour le poisson, pour le nageur, pour le bateau
Qu'elle porte
Et qu'elle emporte.

63                          *Oiseau*

Charmée... Oh! pauvre fille!
Les oiseaux mettent en désordre
Le soleil aveuglant du toit,
Les oiseaux jouent à remplacer
Le soleil plus léger que l'huile
Qui coule entre nous.

64                          *Chien* [I]

Chien chaud,
Tout entier dans la voix, dans les gestes
De ton maître,
Prends la vie comme le vent,
Avec ton nez.

Reste tranquille.

65                      *Chat*

Pour ne poser qu'un doigt dessus
Le chat est bien trop grosse bête.
Sa queue rejoint sa tête,
Il tourne dans ce cercle
Et se répond à la caresse.

Mais, la nuit, l'homme voit ses yeux
Dont la pâleur est le seul don.
Ils sont trop gros pour qu'il les cache
Et trop lourds pour le vent perdu du rêve.

Quand le chat danse
C'est pour isoler sa prison
Et quand il pense
C'est jusqu'aux murs de ses yeux.


66                   *Araignée*

Découverte dans un œuf,
L'araignée n'y entrera plus.


67                   *Mouillé*

La pierre rebondit sur l'eau
La fumée n'y pénètre pas.
L'eau, telle une peau
Que nul ne peut blesser
Est caressée
Par l'homme et par le poisson.

Claquant comme corde d'arc,
Le poisson, quand l'homme l'attrape,

Meurt, ne pouvant avaler
Cette planète d'air et de lumière.

Et l'homme sombre au fond des eaux
Pour le poisson
Ou pour la solitude amère
De l'eau souple et toujours close.


68                      *Patte*


Le chat s'établit dans la nuit pour crier,
Dans l'air libre, dans la nuit, le chat crie.
Et, triste, à hauteur d'homme, l'homme entend
    son cri.


69                    *Vache* [2]


Adieu!
Vaches plus précieuses
Que mille bouteilles de lait,

Précieuses aux jeunes qui se marient
Et dont la femme est jolie,

Précieuses aux vieux avec leur canne
Dont la richesse est chair, lait, terre,

Précieuses à qui veut bien vivre
De la nourriture ordinaire,
Adieu!


70                      *Fuir*


L'araignée rapide,
Pieds et mains de la peur,
Est arrivée.

L'araignée
Heureuse de son poids,
Reste immobile
Comme le plomb du fil à plomb.

Et quand elle repart,
Brisant tous les fils,
C'est la poursuite dans le vide
Qu'il faut imaginer,

Toute chose détruite..

71                *Poule* [2]

Il faut que la poule ponde:
Poule avec ses fruits mûrs.
Poule avec notre gain.

72                *A l'échelle animale*

I

Cette petite tache de lumière dans la campagne
Ce feu du soir est un serpent à la tête froide
La tache de la bête dans un paysage humain
Où tous les animaux sont les mouvements
De la terre bien réelle
Du soleil maigre et pâle
Du soleil gros et rouge
Et de la lune sans passé
Et de la lune à souvenirs

Cette petite tache de lumière cette fenêtre
Éclaire les épaules adorables d'un ours
Et d'un loup de Paris vieux de mille ans

Et d'un furieux sanglier d'aujourd'hui
Et d'un lièvre qui fuit comme un innocent

La forêt voilà la forêt
Malgré la nuit je la vois
Je la touche je la connais
Je fais la chasse à la forêt
Elle s'éclaire d'elle-même
Par ses frissons et par ses voix

Chaque arbre d'ombre et de reflets
Est un miroir pour les oiseaux
Et la rivière la rivière
Dont les poissons sont les bergers
Quelle rivière bien dressée

Voir clair dans l'œil droit des hiboux
Voir clair dans les gouttes de houx
Dans le terrier fourré d'obscurité fondante
Voir clair dans la main des taupes
Dans l'aile étendue très haut
Dans le gui des philosophes
Dans le tout cela des savants
Monde connu et naturel

Voir clair et se reconnaître
Sur la prairie bleue et verte
Où vont chevaux et perdreaux
Sur la plaine blanche et noire
Où vont corbeaux et renards
Voir clair dans le chant des crapauds
Dans le désordre des insectes
Dans les astres de la rosée
Dans les astres des œufs couvés
Dans la chaleur réglée et pure
Dans le vent dur du vieil hiver
Dans un monde mort et vivant

## II

Le poids d'un chien sortant de l'eau
Comme un sourire ému d'une brouille d'amis
Miroirs brisés miroirs entiers

Le poids toujours nouveau
D'une chatte duvet
Les griffes sous la mousse

Et le poids flamboyant
D'une chatte écorchée
Par un fourreau d'aiguilles

Le poids du jour qui réfléchit
Et qui s'arrête comme un âne
A chaque pas

Et je ramasse avec lui
Les miettes de son effort
Sempiternel

D'où sommes-nous sinon d'ici
Et d'ailleurs toujours en butte
A ce compte monotone
D'armées et de solitaires

Bain d'abeilles paravent
De la poussière immuable
Balance des hirondelles
Dans une poitrine vide

Âne chèvre jusqu'à l'herbe
Rat de la poupe à la proue
Rossignol jusqu'au déluge
Jusqu'aux étoiles éteintes

Sont pesants les rongeurs
Pesants comme une horloge
Et les poissons pêchés
Et l'hermine par sa blancheur
Et le lièvre par son repos

Je suis avec toutes les bêtes
Pour m'oublier parmi les hommes

73                 *A l'échelle animale*

### I

Un taureau comme une roue
Loin du sable loin de l'eau
Et dans son œil écarlate
Prend racine la massue

Un taureau tirant à terre
Comme un arc comme une épée
Fendant l'homme en son milieu
Et construisant dans le sang

Les fondations du soleil.

### II

Le beau temps est la proie du vent
L'herbe est la proie des bonnes bêtes

Entre les cornes du taureau
Jaillissait la source du sang

Écumait la source vivante
Les poings serrés sur un trésor

Et la lumière sans passé
Qui ne connaît jamais la mort.

III

Entre les bras ouverts des cornes
Du taureau plume et plomb d'accord
Le soleil tendait son miroir
Aux torches noires de la peur

Gloire un taureau s'en va dans l'herbe
Filer une harmonie de masses
Et sa chair est une bataille
Gagnée d'avance par le cœur.

74                    *D'une bête*

J'aime les bêtes c'est Maïakowski
Qui dit j'aime les bêtes et il a aussitôt envie
De le prouver il leur sourit et il les voit répondre

Nous avions une chienne elle était un peu folle
La tête un peu trop noire pour un corps trop gris
Il a fallu la tuer j'entends car c'est la chasse
A tout moment le coup de feu qui la consume

La source de la vie se courbe sur sa fin
Nous nous courbons chaque jour un peu plus
Sur notre chienne absente notre chienne exigeante.

# APPENDICES

I have used 'Appendices' to describe what follows, because 'Notes' would be misleading. The difficulties which inhere in Éluard's poetry are not ones which can be clarified by the explanation of words, references and allusions; the reading of these poems does not require special kinds of knowledge which an editor can supply. The difficulties to be encountered in Éluard's poems are created by the play of meaning, by syntactical equivocations, by the interferences of different image-fields; in other words, any act of explanation would inevitably entail an act of total interpretation and this is the reader's business rather than an editor's. Instead, the three appendices are intended to provide contextual information, suggestions for an approach to reading and a limited number of skeletal interpretations. In 'Biographical notes' will be found potted lives of the artists involved in the Pictorial section of the anthology. These are designed to give the student a rough background to the artists and to encourage a further exploration of their work; the poems in this section should, in fact, be treated as pretexts for excursions into the contemporary visual arts. Under 'Themes' I have drawn up a list of words which seem to me to represent some of the key threads in Éluard's poetic mentality; and I try briefly to suggest ways in which such words might be intertwined, while warning about the shortcomings of such a list – students may well find that their own idea of what constitutes an 'essential' Éluardian lexicon differs markedly from mine. Finally, 'Interpretations' offers outline readings of some of the poems mentioned in the Introduction.

## APPENDIX I: BIOGRAPHICAL NOTES

The painters are listed in the order in which they appear in the poems.

### *Giorgio de Chirico* (See also Introduction, pp. 21–3)

b. 1888 in Volo, seaside town in Greece. In Munich 1905–9; influence of Böcklin, Stück, Klinger and ideas of Nietzsche, Schopenhauer. Arrived in Paris via Italy, 1911. Attracted friendship and admiration of Apollinaire (theme of mannequin common to both); portrait of Apollinaire 1914. Recalled to Italy (Ferrara) for military service in 1915, but assigned to office job because of illness, and later exempted on neuropsychiatric grounds. The pictorial and theoretical threads of de Chirico's work 1910–17 were gathered together in 1917 under the banner of the 'Scuola Metafisica' which de Chirico established for a short period with Carlo Carrá, the ex-Futurist. After 1920, de Chirico's work reverted to classical and baroque sources, much to the disillusionment of the Surrealists, a disillusionment which peaked in 1928 with the publication of Breton's *Le Surréalisme et la peinture*. But the Surrealists lost none of their enthusiasm for the 1910–18 output, and had a high opinion of de Chirico's novel *Hebdomeros* (1929). De Chirico died in 1978.

### *Pablo Picasso*

b. 1881 in Malaga, Spain. Moved to Paris in 1900, where seventy-five of his works were exhibited by Vollard in 1901. 1901–4: the 'Blue' period – canvases of society's pariahs and unprivileged (the poor, street-players, prostitutes and so on) given a peculiar vulnerability and yet almost metaphysical dignity by the predominant blues. In 1904 the Montmartre tenement known as the 'Bateau-Lavoir' became his studio and equally the meeting-place for a whole group of *avant-garde* artists. 1905–6: the 'Rose' period – softer more decorative treatment, in pinks and greys, of clowns, acrobats and children. Increasing influence of ancient Iberian art and African sculpture: *Les Demoiselles d'Avignon* (1907). Mimetic realism and evocations of mood disappear. 1908: initiated Cubism with Braque, multi-perspectival, abstract, flat. In 1918 he married a dancer, Olga Koklova, and in 1920–1 adopted a monumental 'classical' style in which he executed a series of paintings of women. His relationship with Surrealism was too mercurial to allow any easy identification of influence. In the late 1920s his painting passed through the period of 'metamorphoses', strange forms set in undefined spaces. The Spanish Civil War drew out the expressionist tendencies in his art, not only in *Guernica* (1937), but in the series of weeping women of the same year. After the Second World War, in 1946, he settled in the South of France, shuttling between Golfe-Juan (near Cannes) and the Musée Grimaldi at Antibes. In 1948 he settled at Vallauris and turned to ceramics, while maintaining his remarkable output of paintings, engravings, illustrations and sculpture, up to his death in 1973.

## *André Masson*

b. 1896 in Balagny. Studied in Brussels and Paris. In the early 1920s fell under the spell of the Cubists, particularly the cubism of Juan Gris, but was soon drawn into the Surrealist circle (1925) and became a moving force, with Miró and Ernst, in the development of its automatic, free-associative, non-illusionistic phase, prior to the 1930s (see his sand paintings of 1926–7). His painting of the 1920s portrays a world of generative energies rather than of organized forms. But there is evidence of an equally strong preoccupation with violence and aggression (see his series of fighting animals,

1927–30, and of massacres, 1931–3). By 1929 he had broken with Breton for personal reasons and joined other 'marginal' Surrealists: Leiris, Bataille, Artaud. In Spain 1934–6: insect pictures (1934), propagandist drawings for the Republican cause. On his return to Paris (December 1936), he re-entered the Surrealist circle and developed a figurative vein of fantasy (the 'animated furniture' and 'paroxyst' pictures of 1937–9), without ever renouncing abstract work. The labyrinth myth is central to his work: Theseus is the conscious mind finding its way through the windings of the unconscious towards the irrational source, the Minotaur. In America 1941–5: the organic strain reappeared, and Negro and Red Indian myths became a source of inspiration. Back in France, he settled near Aix in 1947. His work has continued to evolve through a whole sequence of metamorphoses (still-life, Impressionist-style painting, oriental work) while continuing to draw on natural and archetypal imagery. Masson has also designed costumes and sets for theatrical productions, and illustrated literary texts, notably those of Leiris, Gertrude Stein, Robert Desnos and André Malraux.

*Paul Klee*

b. 1879 in Münchenbuchsee, near Bern. After early training in Munich, and travels in Italy, he returned to Bern in 1902 to develop his graphic skills under the influence of artists as diverse as Blake, Goya and Beardsley. In 1906 he went back to Munich where he became familiar with the work of the Impressionists, Van Gogh, Cézanne and Matisse, and in 1911 joined forces with the Expressionists (Macke, Jawlensky, Kandinsky and Marc) exhibiting with them in the third of the *Blaue Reiter* exhibitions (1912); a trip to Tunisia with Macke and an old school-friend, Moilliet (1914), released the colourist in him. 1921–31: he taught at the Bauhaus, first in Weimar, then in Dessau, and at the end of this period proceeded to a chair at the Düsseldorf Academy. His teaching accorded with his own systematic investigation of the specific expressive values of colour and line, and with his belief that creation was as critical an operation as it was instinctive. Harassed by the Nazis, in 1933 he went back to Bern where he spent the rest of his life. He died at Muralte-Lugano in 1940. His work, for all its carefulness of method and vigilant ironies, appeals equally to the unconscious, to childlike fantasy and humorous whimsy. Like the Surrealists, he experimented with automatic techniques and located his products in a world precariously balanced between abstraction and representation. Éluard was in correspondence with him from 1928.

## Max Ernst

b. at Brühl (near Cologne) in 1891. 1914: first contact with Hans Arp. After the First World War, he founded the Dada group of Cologne with Johannes Baargeld, and with Arp produced *Fatagaga* ('*fa*brication de *ta*bleaux *ga*rantis *gazo*-métriques'), a series of collages. In 1922, he settled in Paris, in the same building as Éluard (Saint-Brice); publication with Éluard of *Les Malheurs des immortels* and *Répétitions*. Collaborated on the review *Littérature*; his new friends (Éluard, Breton, Aragon, Soupault, Desnos, Crevel, Péret) figure in his painting *Au rendez-vous des amis* (1922). 1925: participated in first exhibition of Surrealist group and initiated *frottage*, laying paper on a wooden floor, rubbing over it with a pencil and then transmuting the results into precise images in response to their suggestiveness (these first fruits of *frottage* were assembled in *Histoire naturelle*, 1926). He saw *frottage* as an equivalent of automatic writing and adapted it to painting and other media. 1926: collaborated with Miró on the ballet *Roméo et Juliette* for Diaghilev. Published collage-novels: *La Femme 100 têtes* (1929), *Rêve d'une petite fille qui voulut entrer au Carmel* (1930), *Une semaine de bonté* (1934). The later 1920s saw the appearance in his painting of the theme of the forest (forests for him are 'savage and impenetrable, ... swarming, diametrical, negligent, ferocious, fervent and lovable, with neither yesterday nor tomorrow'); and in the 1930s, the image of the city, full of ageless phantoms, petrified, as the forest, preoccupied him. During the Second World War, he found sanctuary in America; he edited the review *V V V* with Breton and Duchamp (1942–4) and developed an automatic painting by oscillation (paint flowing from a swinging can). In 1953, he returned to France. 1954: awarded first prize at the Venice Biennale. Throughout his work, birds – and doves in particular – are a recurrent motif, familiar spirits, forces of regeneration and lyrical serenity; chief among birds is the enigmatic Loplop, his personal muse. He died in 1976.

### *Georges Braque*

b. at Argenteuil in 1882. His apprenticeship in painting was served in a decorator's business. After a youth at Le Havre, he moved to Paris in 1900 and studied at the École des Beaux-Arts and the Académie Humbert. His friendship with Dufy and Othon Friesz introduced him into the Fauve circle, with whom he exhibited in 1906. In 1907, he met Picasso, whose *Les Demoiselles d'Avignon* heralded the geometries and multi-perspectivism of Cubism; working closely with Picasso, he had, by the end of 1909, fully developed his Cubist style: the superimposition of different views of a single object, the translation of spatial relations into purely formal patterns, in short, the analysis of the three-dimensional in two dimensions. In 1912, at a point when Cubism threatened to dissolve the real world into pure abstractions, he introduced new raw materials into his work through collage – paper, bits of wood and cloth, sand and so on. The collaboration with Picasso was interrupted by the outbreak of the First World War, in which he was seriously wounded (1915). After a long convalescence, he resumed painting in 1917, without Picasso, giving light a greater role and endowing the subject with a new stability by locating it more firmly in space; the Cubist inspiration never completely deserted him, but it became increasingly colourful, less analytic and more expressive. His later work is characterized by economy, decorativeness and an ingenuous freshness. He has also left a substantial body of sculpture (animals, birds and fish), plaster reliefs and lithographs. He died in 1963.

## Joan Miró

b. 1893 at Montroig, Catalonia. Potter and sculptor as well as painter. His first paintings derive from his study at the Galí Art Academy in Barcelona (1912–15). He went through Fauvist (1915), Realist (1918, Montroig landscapes) and Cubist (1919) phases, and spent some time in Paris in 1919, where he attended Dadaist meetings and made the acquaintance of Max Jacob and Pierre Reverdy. Thereafter he made annual winter visits to Paris, first occupying a studio next to Masson's and then, 1927, moving to Montmartre where his neighbours were Ernst, Magritte, Arp and Éluard. Throughout the 1920s, he benefited from the stimulus of Surrealism; his biomorphic shapes, brilliant primary colours, childlike dream-constructions and warm humour led Breton to call him 'the most "surrealist" of us all'. After a sequence of Dutch interiors (1928), he turned to collages and imaginary portraits (1929). 1932 found him designing for Léonide Massine's ballet *Jeux d'enfants*, followed by experiments with watercolours, pastels, paintings on sandpaper and copper, gouaches, murals. His style underwent a gradual simplification. During the war years, spent at Palma, Mallorca, he executed his gouache series *Constellations* and from 1944 was working in collaboration with the Spanish ceramist José Artigas. The 1940s and 1950s saw the completion of large murals at Harvard (Harkness Commons Dining Room), Cincinnati (Hilton Hotel) and Paris (UNESCO building). There has always been a strong calligraphic presence in his work, part of a desire to minimize the distinction between painting and poetry. He has illustrated texts by Tzara, Char, Leiris and Crevel.

## Yves Tanguy

b. 1900 in Paris. Of Breton origin, he spent some time in the merchant navy travelling to England, Spain, Portugal, Africa and South America. He did no painting until his return to Paris in 1922, where a de Chirico in the window of the Galerie Paul Guillaume (1923) acted upon him with all the force of a revelation (Breton had first encountered de Chirico's work in much the same way). At this time he shared a house with the poet Jacques Prévert, an old friend, and Marcel Duchamp. In 1925, he joined the Surrealist movement and found his style, suddenly, in 1927, after absorbing the work of Miró, Masson and Ernst. With the outbreak of the Second World War, he moved to America and lived in Woodbury, Connecticut, with his wife, the painter Kay Sage, until his death in January 1955; he took American citizenship in 1948. His work is characterized by an increasing attention to the mineral world, by an illusionist technique, by spatial and gravitational ambiguity (the dissolving of land into sky in deep space, objects which might be floating or resting on a surface), dramatization of shadow, lunar or subaquatic atmosphere. Many of the shapes which haunt his deathly landscapes are perhaps reminiscent of Breton dolmens and menhirs.

## Salvador Dali

b. 1904 in Figueras, Catalonia. His early enthusiasms were for Cubism, Futurism and Metaphysical painting (de Chirico); but at the same time he cultivated a meticulously illusionistic realism and interested himself in the photographic arts (later he was to make two films with Luis Buñuel: *Le Chien andalou* (1929) and *L'Age d'or* (1931) ). After exhibitions of paintings in Barcelona (1925) and Madrid (1926), he joined the Surrealists in Paris in 1929 and married Éluard's former wife, Gala. It was under his influence that Surrealist painting took its 'representational' direction in the 1930s. His own 'paranoiac-critical' method led him into explorations of hallucinatory experiences and abnormal psychological states. When, in the late 1930s, he returned to the Italian Renaissance for models, he was attacked by Breton for being an academic reactionary. He moved to the United States in 1940 and turned his attention to religious themes, a vein he continued to exploit on his return to Spain after the war (*The Crucifixion* 1951; *The Last Supper* 1955). Dali has remained the showman of Surrealism, flamboyant, fantastical, elusively ironic, and often unnervingly serious.

## *Man Ray*

b. 1890 in Philadelphia. Spent the years between 1897 and 1921 in New York, before settling in Paris. It was in New York that he made the acquaintance of Marcel Duchamp and Francis Picabia, with whom he founded the New York Dada movement during the First World War. He showed work in the first Surrealist exhibition, of 1925, and turned to photography – principally, at first, as a means of livelihood. Rather like Picasso, he was an unremittingly experimental artist; he never wished to settle into a style, but always to be as different from himself as possible. Hence the great variety of his output: Cubist paintings, Dadaist objects, Surrealist photographs and films (for example *Emak Bakia* (1926), *L'Étoile de mer* (1926), *Les Mystères du Château de Dés* (1928) ), and, throughout, many mixed-media products. He died in 1976.

## *René Magritte*

b. 1898 in Lessives (Belgium). Studied at the Académie des Beaux-Arts in Brussels. After interesting himself in Cubism and Futurism, he turned to Surrealism in 1925, largely under the impetus of de Chirico's influence. He became very closely acquainted with Éluard and Breton when he moved to Paris in 1926, though it was particularly to Belgian Surrealism that he devoted his energies. He returned to Brussels in 1931, where, a few years later, he was to exercise a decisive influence on his compatriot Paul Delvaux. His profoundly immobile pictures, set, like so many Surrealist paintings, in disturbingly boundless spaces, owe nothing to automatism or chance; painted with academic illusionism, they explore the nature of illusion and the ways we interpret visual evidence. His understated method only seems to intensify the incongruity of the juxtaposed elements in his pictures. And the disquiet of the spectator is merely increased by the obliquity of his enigmatic titles (compare with Tanguy's titles) which seem to ride off at tangents to the depicted image. He died in Brussels in 1967.

### *Marc Chagall* (see also Introduction, pp. 24–5, and Appendix III, pp. 127–8)

b. 1887 in Vitebsk (Russia). Studied in St Petersburg (1907–10), partly at the school founded by the theatrical designer Leon Bakst, and visited Paris (1910–14), making contact with the artistic *avant-garde* (Apollinaire, Cendrars, Jacob, Modigliani, Delaunay). He returned to Vitebsk to teach (1914–22). The Russian Revolution brought him a commissarship for the fine arts in Vitebsk district, thanks to Lunacharsky, whom he had met in Paris in 1912. He resigned from this post after a while and busied himself with theatrical design (Yiddish Theatre) in Moscow. In spring 1923, he returned to France, after a stay in Berlin, but left in 1940, taking up an invitation, in 1941, from the Museum of Modern Art in New York. He came back to France from America in 1947 and settled permanently at Vence in 1949. His work has never lost the traces of its Russian Jewish origins; but angels, violinists, cows, cockerels, moons, lovers, acrobats, elements of a specific environment, achieve mythic force through their colourful persistence, and through their fusion of past, present and future in a world which is open to dream and desire as much as to memory, and is freed from the pull of gravity and spatial restriction.

## Fernand Léger

b. 1881 in Argetan. Entered the École des Beaux-Arts briefly in 1903 and in 1908 moved to a studio in 'La Ruche', an artists' community of cosmopolitan variety in the passage de Dantzig. He became friendly with, among others, Cendrars, Jacob, André Salmon, Apollinaire, Reverdy, Picasso, and Delaunay. He developed his own form of Cubism after 1909, a cubism of solid, heavy masses, highly coloured. During the First World War, he 'discovered' the attractions of the machine and the machine-made, and from this emerged a classicism of the mechanized age (1920), carefully ordered, monumental, and permeated by a sense of human solidarity. This development also owed something to his meeting with Le Corbusier, who introduced him to the challenge of the mural. In the later 1920s, he adapted his painting to Surrealism, but paid more attention to the formal, rather than psychological, implications of incongruously juxtaposed objects. During the Second World War, he found refuge in New York where he took up the practice of dissociating colour from outline. On his return to France in 1946, he concentrated on the 'public' function of his art and busied himself with theatrical design, mosaics, stained glass, ceramics and murals. It was in 1953 that he composed his *poème-object* on Éluard's line: 'Liberté, j'écris ton nom'. These later works perfectly embody his project for a post-Cubist art that would be, above all, an art for the people. He died in 1955.

### APPENDIX II: THEMES

To encourage, and perhaps facilitate, thematic explorations of Éluard's poetry, I have made a list of some of the dominant lexical items in the anthologized poems. The selection has not been made on a quantitative basis: that is to say, I have not fed the poems into a computer and listed those words which occur with the greatest frequency. Quite intentionally, my choice is part-instinctive, part-empirical, part-haphazard; intentionally, because I wish to court dissatisfaction and stimulate further investigation. Such an undertaking inevitably raises questions of a theoretical nature, some of which are listed below. The student would perhaps do well to ponder these before making use of the lexicon.

(i) Are the words which occur most frequently in a poet's work necessarily the most important? Are these the words to which the poems themselves actually give prominence? A poet may, after all, seek to give a special status to certain words by using them only sparingly and besides, the frequency of a word in a poet's lexicon may only indicate its frequency in general usage; we would not be surprised to find that Éluard uses the word 'feuille' more often than the word 'aiguille', for it merely confirms what we already expect about the frequency of these words in common usage.

(ii)  Are we right to assume that thematic material is located primarily in nouns, adjectives and verbs? The list on pages 119–20 tacitly reinforces this assumption. But, as the Introduction and Interpretations which follow try to suggest, words of apparently minor grammatical status – articles, prepositions (look at Éluard's use of 'à travers', 'autour de', 'devant', for example) and other particles – may carry a burden of signification far greater than that implied by their syntactic function, a signification which indeed relates to thematic concerns. Pronouns and adverbs are equally worthy of attention (see 'tous/tout' and 'toujours' for instance).

(iii) Are there some words that have privileged relationships with others? There are obvious logical connections between 'reflets', 'regards' and 'yeux'. But are there connections between, say, 'feu' and 'arbre', or 'rire' and 'rêve' which considerations of frequency alone might overlook?

I must repeat that my selection is a *selection* and is thus guilty of omissions (for example verbs, abstract nouns, cognates, antonyms). But lack of space prevents comprehensiveness and perhaps these omissions will be rectified by the further explorations of dissatisfied readers.

*The Lexicon* (A selection of fifty words; the numbers after each word refer to the numbers of the poems in which that word is to be found; each item allows, where relevant, for feminine and plural forms.)

aiguille: 11, 52, 56, 72

aile: 7, 21, 28, 29, 36, 45, 46, 49, 51, 57, 72

arbre: 10, 13, 23, 42, 54, 56, 72

bateau: 21, 29, 41, 52

bonheur: 2, 3, 4, 9, 10, 15, 16, 53

bouche: 7, 22, 30, 38, 41, 52, 57

bras: 14, 15, 33, 34, 52, 73

désir: 17, 18, 20, 41, 42, 51, 52

doux/douceur/doucement: 3, 10, 21, 28, 29, 30, 34, 46, 59, 62

enfant/enfance/enfantin: 2, 9, 10, 13, 15, 16, 17, 27, 28, 30, 32, 36, 42, 53, 59

espoir: 1, 4, 11, 15, 18, 22, 32, 38, 42

étoile/astre: 11, 21, 22, 29, 36, 44, 46, 47, 51, 52, 72

faim/affamé: 8, 11, 40

fenêtre/vitre: 13, 20, 23, 24, 72

feu: 9, 10, 11, 29, 32, 36, 39, 41, 42, 50, 72, 74

feuille: 9, 21, 23, 25, 27, 36, 44, 49, 51, 54, 56

frère: 7, 11, 15, 32

goutte: 7, 9, 29, 33, 72

hirondelle: 4, 42, 53, 72

larme: 1, 9, 14, 36, 40, 47, 52, 53

léger: 9, 33, 49, 54, 63

lèvre: 9, 10, 25, 32, 33, 42, 55

main: 2, 9, 16, 19, 20, 23, 24, 25, 27, 32, 38, 41, 42, 44, 46, 51, 52, 53, 56, 70, 72

miroir: 22, 28, 36, 43, 44, 54, 56, 72, 73

mot/parole: 15, 20, 23, 30, 34, 35, 41, 42, 43

mur: 9, 14, 35, 43, 44, 48, 65

neige: 10, 28, 32, 40, 43, 45, 52, 55

nuit/nocturne: 1, 7, 8, 10, 14, 16, 18, 21, 23, 24, 27, 28, 29, 30, 31, 32, 35, 37, 38, 39, 40, 41, 42, 45, 48, 50, 51, 52, 55, 58, 65, 68, 72

œil(yeux): 2, 11, 13, 14, 15, 16, 17, 19, 21, 22, 23, 25, 28, 29, 30, 32, 35, 36, 37, 38, 41, 42, 44, 47, 48, 49, 51, 52, 53, 54, 56, 65, 72, 73

oiseau: 7, 23, 27, 28, 29, 32, 33, 34, 41, 48, 49, 52, 55, 57, 63, 72

ombre: 10, 12, 19, 20, 25,

\*    \*    \*

The works of Raymond Jean (1968) and Jean-Pierre Richard (1964), listed in the Select Bibliography, contain very helpful analyses of Éluardian themes and their inter-relationships; their findings often overlap and reinforce each other. 'Bateau' (or 'barque'), for example, is at one and the same time a womb-like place of refuge and an agent of exploration and forward momentum – the boat pushes back the storm. The movement of the boat also has a strong sensual charge: it glides effortlessly over the water and penetrates space, as if pushing it open. 'Vitre' is something both resistant and transparent, a screen which reveals. But it is often presented as an *empty* mirror, allowing the face or the look to be dissipated rather than be gathered up and returned in a reflection. 'Fenêtre' is, of course, closely con-nected with 'vitre', but it is not so much a surface as a frame, which provides privileged access to a newly discovered world. Thus like the 'vitre', the window is associated with feelings of expectation, anticipation of revelation, often cruelly disappointed. Immobility, recalcitrance, opacity, these are the principles with which the stone ('pierre'/'caillou') opposes the transparency, amenability and mobility of the Éluardian ideal. Sometimes, however, the obstinate hardness of the stone is called upon to give density to an identity, to celebrate its particularity and difference, while this in itself may be part of a process of gradual absorption into a larger element. Much has been said of the significance of eyes in the Introduction. The closing of the eyelids ('paupières') takes the images of the eye inwards; but the eyelids can equally fix the image on the eye itself, hold it as if captive. And inasmuch as closed eyes are the eyes of sleep and dream, the eyelids are the junction of two realities, the very point of transformation of one reality into another. Both 'rire' and 'sourire' have to do with the resonant eruption of a life-force, elemental and youthful. Laughter establishes an intimate and radiating contact with the outside world; it is an act of trust and of spontaneous pleasure in existence; it is a communication of strength, or, in amorous contexts, the very sound of terrestrial happiness. If much of Éluard's imagery seems to be concerned with the reconciliation of the transparent and the opaque, of limpidity and plenitude, then, Richard argues, 'sang' is a crucial bridge, blood which, for him, is 'cette chair active et fluide, ce mouvement-substance' (p. 110); and he goes on to show how its palpitating characteristics mate blood to wind, laughter, heat.

In attempting thematic interpretation of this nature, we must remember three things. First, a word will achieve thematic significance more by the constancy or peculiarity of its use than by the consistency of its meaning; words become themes not by virtue of their singleness of purpose or semantic stability, but by their power of attraction, their ability to embed themselves in networks of relationship, as versatile and developing elements. Consequently, and second, no thematic account of a poet's work will be adequate if it tries to impose thematic *données* on every context; the suggestions provided above as to the significance of certain themes need not necessarily hold good for all appearances of those themes, for themes are extremely elastic fields of meaning. Third, and relatedly, themes are as much subject to acoustic considerations, of the kind dealt with in the Typographical and Prosodic section, as any other words; that is to say, the phonetic constituents of a thematic word may be an essential key to its semantic kinships and area of reference. Some illustration of this last remark is to be found in the work of Henri Meschonnic (see Select Bibliography).

In his study of the collection *La Vie immédiate*, Meschonnic examines the acoustic reverberations of 'orage', a word with both destructive and fecundating associations; he notes its consonantal affiliations with words like 'brise', 'rire', 'brassage', 'germe', and particularly with 'neige', which itself has deep, though non-acoustic, ties with 'oiseaux'; so that he is able to speak of 'la complexité florale-ailée-neigeuseféminine de l'orage' in the opening stanza of 'Une pour toutes' (p. 68). It is the changing life and ingredients of such constellations of words that must occupy the thematic analyst. In drawing up an essential Éluardian lexicon, I have not sought to isolate and determine units of meaning so much as to alert the reader to those words which seem to exist in peculiarly potent, almost magnetic, relationships with one another.

## APPENDIX III: INTERPRETATIONS

The poems are listed in the order in which they are treated in the Introduction.

### *Couvre-feu* (p. 52)

Is this poem an apoplogy for defensive self-indulgence or a defiant affirmation of channels of communication which no prohibitions can close? The title itself participates in this ambiguity: it is the curfew, confinement to the house, the covering of the fire, but equally it is the extinguishing of a light to find intimacy, it is the covering or concealment of a figurative fire, a fire which no curfews will subdue. And so the very restriction of freedom ironically generates the freedom to love. The verse-form, assonated (rhymed) decasyllables, takes us towards popular poetry, a direction reinforced by the colloquial 'Que voulez-vous', and towards the *laisse*, the stanza of the medieval French epic (*chanson de geste*), whose lines are also usually decasyllabic and related by terminal assonance. The poem is thus wrapped in a crypto-mantle of corporateness and national memory. And it demonstrates, too, how public attitudes can emerge from privacies intensely pursued, how human solidarity depends on the defence of very personal happinesses.

The poet's ability to wriggle out of repression derives from the resourcefulness, even duplicity, of language. The 'nous' of lines 2 and 6 is at once the couple and the larger community, and while the 'nous' of the final line is more evidently the couple, it, too, by virtue of previous usage, finds itself endowed with a certain elasticity. Line 6 will also remind us that military language is a commonplace source of metaphor for amatory verse, and as this awareness is released in us, so the military might of the occupying force is absorbed into, and subjugated by, the more fundamental, unchanging act of loving. If 'désarmés' lures us towards a more precious and euphemistic lexicon, so 'affamée', in both its literal and figurative aspects, confronts us with needs more imperious and earthy ('elle', though ostensibly referring to 'la ville', might be seen to imply the poet's shadowy partner). Thus, out of the uniformity of the poem's formulation and the stern anonymity of repression, slips a buoyancy, a versatility of insinuation, which will not be subdued. And this refusal to surrender finds its clearest expression in the change of tense in the final line. From the inertia of passive verb forms and the unspecified and attritional duration of the imperfect, we move to an active verb, to a perfect tense, to a tense of past action, but reaching forward into a present animated by that past action; and the reflexive form of this verb gives a wonderfully insistent existence to 'nous'.

## Gabriel Péri (p. 59)

Gabriel Péri – and let us not forget that 'péri' is both the past participle of 'périr' and a genie of Persian mythology, originally malevolent but later beneficent – was a member of the Central Committee of the Communist Party (1929), editor of L'Humanité, and later vice-president of the Foreign Commission of the Chamber of Deputies. He was shot by the Nazis on 15 December 1941. The poem is a setting for his name, actually seems to demand his name, as a missing key which alone can explain and subsume the concerted rhyme-phrases 'ouverts à la vie', 'hait les fusils', 'contre l'oubli', all proffering the 'i' sound, as do many subsequent lines ('vivre', 'ami', 'découvrir', 'liberté', 'gentillesse' and so on), a sound of which Péri is, as it were, the chosen fount and keeper. The name 'Péri' is also summoned by the procession of words in the final stanza. On the one hand, these are primarily abstract and common nouns which are manifest, irreplaceable and occupy their own special space; on the other, they are a privileged but unutterable selection, first of the names of flowers and fruits and then of names of places and people. If these names cannot be uttered, it is because without Péri's name a gap persists between them and those moral qualities (love, justice, liberty and so on) which give them meaning. And once Péri's name has emphatically installed itself, so we recognize him with immediate intimacy ('Tutoyons-le') and through him recognize each other.

### 'La courbe de tes yeux...' (p. 65)

The first line could well be taken as a metaphysical conceit: the image of the loved one's eyes as orbiting planets ensnaring the lover's heart in their trajectories:

La courbe de tes yeux fait le tour de mon cœur

But the 'courbe', which we understand at first as 'flight-path', must also be thought of as a choreography ('rond de danse'), as a yielding shape ('rond de douceur'), as an en-circling movement round the linearity of time which gives it a certain luminosity ('auréole du temps'), and as a curve along which we can move comfortingly backwards and forwards ('berceau nocturne et sûr'). In typical fashion, Éluard accumulates an appositional sequence which makes the movement of the poem diffusive, as association shifts and melts into association. Indeed the appositional relationship of the phrases may convince us that this process is close to instantaneousness, that the movement through these phrases is of an increasingly inclusive and non-defining kind – the absence of articles in the third line is some indication of that. And so the lines are not so much a series of compliments paid to a person as a celebration of the energy released by an attraction, a declaration of the origins of that energy.

The first stanza ends with two peculiarly prosaic, almost graceless lines which date the poet's conscious existence from his being seen by the loved one; eyes confer vision on those they look at, eyes gather reflections from those they are seen by. These two rhyming lines are a moment of simple, irreducible truth, a recognition that the desire to celebrate grows not from the beauties of the loved one, but from the acquisition of a new knowledge of the world and of a new ability to integrate the self into it.

The second and third stanzas form a continuous whole, an enumeration which, with its ecstatic absence of articles, takes over where the previous sequence left off. And here, too, we find an insistent use of the genitive:

> Feuilles *de* jour et mousse *de* rosée
> Roseaux *du* vent...

where the preposition 'de' signifies a close but unspecified relationship ('de' – possessed by, made of, belonging to, in proximity to?) and shuffles priorities and meanings (which of the pair pivoting round the 'de' is the major term, which the attribute, and which the literal, which the figurative?). But these questions are only evidence of a perfect reciprocity between the nouns, themselves loving couples. The textural consistency of these last two stanzas is borne out by the regularity of the decasyllable and the recurrence of unelided terminal mute 'e's' ('feuill*e*s', 'mouss*e*', 'sourir*e*s', 'ail*e*s', 'mond*e*', 'sourc*e*s', 'un*e*', 'paill*e*', 'comm*e*', 'coul*e*') which make for a yielding, resilient verbal surface and for a rhythmic sinuousness, softly enfolding the poem's contents.

As these stanzas unfold, so the scale of things referred to expands: sky, sea and finally stellar spaces ('sur la paille des astres'). The closely-knit rhyme-structure of the first stanza – two couplets, 'cœur/douceur' and 'vécu/vu', with 'sûr' acting as an acoustic bridge between them – is gradually loosened and the acoustic structures dispersed, though animated by distant echoes (douceur/couleur/pur; vécu/parfumés/ lumière/pur; astres/regards and so on) And the sensations themselves are of a dispersed or dispersive nature: insubstantial, ubiquitous perfumes ('sourires parfumés', 'parfums éclos...), the light of the lovers' visibility disseminated by bird-flight ('ailes couvrant le monde de lumière', 'couvée d'aurores'). But all this expansion finds its home in the synthesizing phrase 'Le monde entier', to which, as it turns out, the preceding sequence of nominal phrases is in apposition.

### A Marc Chagall (p. 94)

The first stanza is remarkable for the indefiniteness or absence of its articles. This fact together with the alternative and equivocating, rather than additional, form of coordination ('ou' rather than 'et') promotes the same sense of weightless purity of being as in a Chagall painting. The structure of the third stanza is similar to that of the first: each first line contains four nouns in two pairs ('Âne ou vache/coq ou cheval'; 'L'or de l'herbe/le plomb du ciel'); each second line is a qualification of the first, with one nominal unit; each third line has two nominal units in enumerative sequence, and the fourth lines share acoustic features, namely a common 4+4 rhythm and phonetic parallels – 'D*ans*eur ag*i*le ave*c* *s*a femme'/'Le *sang s'iri*se le *cœur* tinte' (the two third lines also have a 4+4 rhythmic outline and phonetic points of contact in s, z (phonetic) ā, o, which relate them to the fourth lines). These structural similarities have an integrative effect, as though two panels were being symmetrically drawn towards the centre-piece of a triptych, the first of the one-line stanzas (l.5) on the couple, participating, too, in its acoustic structure:

C*ou*ple tr*em*pé *dan*s *s*on prin*tem*ps          (4+4)

(The phonetic interconnections are, of course, much more complicated than these few observations indicate.)

But the saturation of the third stanza by the definite article *is* a new departure; while the first stanza is a neutral reunion of unspecified 'familiars', the third is a careful demarcation of areas of intense colour and light. The play of articles here acts as a kind of literary equivalent of a pictorial experience. Motifs in a picture become *agents* by virtue of spatial relations and colouristic emphases, just as a noun becomes a protagonist in a specific pattern by assuming the definite article. Items in the pictorial world of Chagall and the literary world of Éluard often come to us without allegiances or ostensible function; innocently they enjoy their confident autonomy, their untroubled availability. But they are also propelled by forces larger than they are – colour, line, rhythm, word-music – and these are simply the embodiments of desires, dreams and fears that have not yet come fully to consciousness. This discovery of a function, of a coherence in dream, is borne out by the syntactical expansiveness and confidence of the final stanza, with its image of the marriage of the human, the vegetal and the cosmic in a state of uninterrupted wakefulness. The final stanza presents us with a world taking shape, emerging from the dark, and generated by a consciousness greater than the dark; that consciousness is the *original* of all consciousnesses, the all-reflective consciousness of the couple:

Uncouple le premier reflet

## *D'une bête* (p. 106)

The laconic attitude and lack of syntactic connectives within this poem transform what might have been mere anecdote into something altogether more interrogative and inexplicable, as though the poet had brushed with some impersonal mystery. The second stanza, in particular, with its repeated, ironically understated 'un peu' and its casually interpolated 'j'entends', seems distant, even offhand. But the poet's closeness to the bitch is not left in any doubt in the final stanza: the bitch's madness, manifest in the second stanza as much in her strangely ill-assorted coat (line 5) as in her gun-dog obsessions and hallucinations, becomes part of her restiveness in death, her refusal to be forgotten; if she was demanding in her lifetime, she is equally so in her death. The downward curve ('La source de la vie se courbe sur sa fin') which is the trajectory of life, is also a bending movement of warmth and solicitude, as though memory intensified with time; the bitch is an increasingly strong magnet. And the 'un peu' in the adverbial phrase 'un peu plus' is not, as in the second stanza, an 'un peu' of ironic disavowal or non-commitment or of incipient contradiction, but an observation of integrated gradualism. The very oddness of the bitch and the tyrannies of her imagination make her unique in the poet's affections.

The whole account is presided over by the almost epigraphic first stanza. The words and example of the Revolutionary Soviet poet Vladimir Mayakovsky (1893–1930) are, as it were, the target and undercurrent of the poem, attitudes with which the poem sets out to converge. And it is important that these words and this example come from beyond the poet, can function as an unobtrusive imperative for the poem; in this way, the poem gathers itself into a larger pattern and makes itself the servant of an appeal to let animals enter our existences on their own terms.

## L'Extase (p. 78)

This is a poem in which 'devant' is transformed, in the final line, into 'dans', in which a situation of *vis-à-vis* culminates in an immersion. As so frequently in Éluard, the ecstasy of love is a complex play of reciprocities finally yielding itself up to a perfect coincidence. Before the lover can allow this mutuality to become a unity, what must be realized is the loved one's ability to gather and redefine a *total* world and the lover's ability to absorb this world and find his own reflection in it, so that the internal and the external become interchangeable.

The poem opens with an alexandrine, but a three-measure alexandrine, tentative, unbalanced, uneven in pace (2+6+4). (My observations on the versification of this poem do not always square with those of C.H. Wake – see Select Bibliography.) Without the structural *point de repère* of a medial caesura, we are cast adrift into a rhythmically amorphous landscape which has yet to take shape. But the alexandrine is not so much amorphous as polymorphous, susceptible of many different rhythmic segmentations; and, in fact, this first line has the effect of making possible the third line, with its stable, measured 3+3+3+3 structure, and the following sequence of equally firmly caesuraed alexandrines (lines 4–6). Interspersed with the poem's alexandrines are six octosyllables, more impatient, crisper, three of which have the achieved equilibrium of a 4+4 pattern; and these three lines are the lines of 'feu' (lines 2, 13, 21), the force of transubstantiation and consummation. There are in addition two hexasyllables (lines 14–15) and two decasyllables (lines 9,17) and, more worthy of attention perhaps, two sixteen-syllable lines (lines 8, 16) both of which express moments of self-extension. The first of these is into a vast and featureless space which threatens effacement of the self, and the second into an equally vast space, but one in which all directions answer one another, a space of plenitude where the self is present to itself at all points. Both these lines have the same 4+4+4+4 structure, that is, the structure which synthesizes the perfectly balanced octosyllable (4+4) and the most regular version of the trimetric alexandrine (line 19):

Et le soleil au bout de tout venant de tout        (4+4+4)

and which gives freest rein to the four-syllable measure, the dominant measure of the poem (for example 'ce paysage', 'où tout remue', 'où des miroirs', 'Belles raisons', 'où la nature', 'Bonne raison', 'identifiée', 'Second bourgeon' and so on). Essentially, then, Éluard is using regular lines in irregular combinations, and occasionally transgressing the conventional rhythmic maximum of twelve syllables. But it

is clear that those kinds of relationship which are character-
istic of the couple – relationships of complementarity, reci-
procity, equivalence, inversion, difference in resemblance –
are particularly suited to the parisyllabic line and to the
parisyllabic line in particular which has a binary structure by
virtue either of a medial caesura (the major structural division
in the alexandrine) or of a single medial *coupe* (the line of
demarcation between rhythmic measures), as in the 4+4
octosyllables.